A CODE OF
PRACTICE FOR
MUSLIMS IN THE WEST

Abdul Hãdi al-Hakím

A Code of Practice for Muslims in the West

in accordance with the edicts of
Ayatullãh al-udhma As-Sayyid
Ali al-Husaini as-Seestãni

Translated by
Sayyid Muhammad Rizvi

Edited by
Najim al-Khafaji

Imam Ali^(a.s.) Foundation
London ◆ UK

Written by: Abdul Hadi al-Hakim
Translated by: Sayyid Muhammad Rizvi
Edited by: Najim al-Khafaji

Published by:

Imam Ali$^{(a.s.)}$ Foundation

Liaison office of Grand Ayatullah
as-Sayyid As-Seestãni
5 Sneyd Road,
Willesden Green,
London NW2 6AL, U.K.

Charity No. 1075650

Tel: (+44) 208-452-8270
Fax: (+44) 208-830-6858
E-Mail: questions@seestani.org
Web: hhtp://www.seestani.org

© Copyright 1999 Imam Ali Foundation
First Published in 1999

*ISBN:*1-902268-02-4

Table of Contents

PART ONE
FIQHUL 'IBĀDĀT'
LAWS ON ACTS OF WORSHIP

PART TWO
FIQHUL MU'ĀMALĀT
LAWS ON MUNDANE ASPECTS OF LIFE

Editor's Note

This book is the second in its league. It is yet another contribution of the author, as-Sayyid Abdul Hadi al-Hakim, after the publication of the translation of his book *alfatawal muyessarah - Jurisprudence Made Easy*, to the effort of making the body of fiqh (jurisprudence) easier for the layman to come to grips with.

Translating such work is a challenging task. Yet the translator, as-Sayyid Mohammad Rizvi, has done a great job. However, where I saw the reader's interest is better served, I have made some changes. The title of the book now reads, *A Code of Practice for Muslims in the West*. To avoid repetition, I decided to collate the translator's footnotes, dealing with clarifying the meanings of the Arabic terms, as well as some other "Frequently Used Terms" under one title, "Glossary ".

I must stress, though, that throughout the process of making these changes, and others for that matter, I was in close consultation with both the author and the publishers, Imarn Ali Foundation, UK, London.

I pray to Allah, the Exalted to forgive any inadvertent mistake or error of judgement I any have made in the course of editing the book. I also implore Him to make this work of mine a step towards attaining His approval, that He accepts it favourably and make it of use.

Najim al-Khafaji, BA

Translator's Preface

In the name of Allãh, the Beneficent, the Merciful.
May Allãh send His blessings upon Muhammad and his progeny.

Writing the manuals of Islamic laws for use by Muslims is an evolutionary process, reflecting the change in lifestyles and the relevance (or the lack of it) of certain problems and issues that vary from time to time and place to place. The spirit and the purpose remain constant but the style and the format change.

In the present century we first saw the widely used *Tawdíhu 'l-Masã'il* in Persian (also known as *risãla-e 'amaliyya*), and then came the *Minhãju 's-Sãlihiyn* in Arabic by the late Ayatullãh al-Hakím (which was later expanded by the late Ayatullãh al-Khû'í and even further improved by Ayatullãh as-Sistãni). In mid seventies, the late Ayatullãh Sayyid Muhammad Bãqir as-Sadr brought about a completely new style in his *al-Fatãwa al-Wãdiha*.

The present book, *al-Fiqh lil Mughtaribín* by Hujjatul Islam Sayyid 'Abdul Hãdi al-Hakím, is a further development in the same line of change and continuity. Sayyid 'Abdul Hãdi's distinction is that he has focused on the problems and issues faced by the Muslims in the West, formulated those questions, and compiled their answers without going into details that can be easily obtained from other commonly used sources of Islamic laws. And so it was indeed a great pleasure when I was asked to undertake the translation of this book into English.

A Note on Translation: I have been quite liberal while translating the author's Introduction but had to strictly abide

by the wording and expressions as they appeared in the
original in the latter and the major part of the book. This was
done to ensure the accuracy in conveying the views of the
Grand Ayatullāh as-Sistāni.

This translation is based on the first Arabic edition of 1998
but with quite a few changes and amendments done by the
Fatwa Committee of the Office of Ayatullāh as-Sistāni in
Qum. And so those who would compare this translation with
the first Arabic edition should keep this fact in mind. The
changes were of various length and nature: in some instances,
words, phrases and sentences were changed or added to further
explain the problem;[1] in some cases, the rulings have
changed;[2] and in three cases, the items were deleted
completely.[3]

Moreover, in some instances I had asked for further
elaboration that was kindly provided by the Committee.[4] I
have also taken the liberty of changing the placement of
certain rulings so that similar issues are found in the same
section. For the same reason, in Part Two, I have switched the
sequence of two chapters: Chapter 8 ("Youths' Issues") and
Chapter 9 ("Women's Issues) since women's issues are much
closer to issues of Chapter 7 on "Marriage". Interestingly this
is the order that the author himself has listed pages 31 and 136
of the Arabic but has somehow changed it in the final printing.
I have written some footnotes to clarify the meaning and have

---

[1] See for example items 16m 20, 23, 29-30 on p. 37-39; item 11, p. 56;
item 96, p. 100; item 178, p. 149; item 301, p. 203; item 383, p. 251.
All page numbers in this note refer to the first Arabic edition.

[2] See, for example, item 114 on p. 110 on sighting of the new moon.

[3] See item 218 (p. 168), item 285 (p. 191), and item 269 (p. 187) in the
first edition.

[4] See item 115 in this translation on the criterion of following the moon
sighted in a city west of your own city.

also added a short list of "Frequently Used Terms" at the beginning of each chapter.

I pray to Almight Allãh to accept this work as a humble attempt in simplifying His laws for the Muslims in non-Muslim societies, and may He reward the author and grant long life to the Ayatullãh as-Sistãni on whose expert opinion this book is based.

Toronto

Sayyid Muhammad Rizvi
Shawwal 1419 / February 1999

Author's Preface

In the name of Allāh, the Beneficent, the Merciful

It is a pleasure for me to present to the respected readers my book, *al-Fiqh lil Mughtaribín,* according to the views: of his eminence Grand Ayatullāh as-Sayyid 'Ali al-Hussaini as-Seestāni (May Allāh prolong his blessed presence among us).

This book is the first attempt at writing Islamic laws For Muslims who have settled in non-Muslim Contries. Muslims who were compelled to leave their countries, and the places where they grew up, and had to migrate to non-Muslim countries in which they now live under different laws and systems, dissimilar values and rules, and unfamiliar customs and habits. The modes of conduct and manners of the host societies are greatly at variance with what the guests were used to; there is a wide gulf between their own upbringing and the values of the host countries. Conceqneutly, new problems have emerged and a number of questions arose that called for answers — answers that would clarify the ambigious, enlighten the obscure, guide the stray, and brighten the darkness.

From this came the need for writing a book that would deal with the various practical problems of immigrant Muslims, and provide answers and present solutions for them.

It was agaist this background that *al-Fiqh lil Mughtaribín* was written with a detailed introduction, followed by two parts with each part branching out into various chapters which contain new questions, issues that had not been charted before, and problems that have not been discussed in most Manuals of Islamic Laws and other commonly used books of Islamic Jurisprudence. Hopefully these parts and chapters will act as a stimulus for further questions that the learned reader may raise; and I will be greatly pleased to receive those queries so that they may be included with their answers in future editions, *insha Allāh*.

Islamic Laws for Muslims in non-Muslim Countries is the third attempt following two other books *"al-Fatāwa al-Muyassara"* (Jurisprudence Made Easy) and *"al-Muntakhab mina 'l-Masā'ili 'l-Muntakhabah"* (Current Legal Issues) through which I hope to have contributed to the process of making Islamic laws accessible, and endear them, to lay People. If I have succeeded in my aim, all praise is due to Allāh; and if have not, it is sufficient that I have tried *"and my success is not but from Allāh, and in Him I place my trust and to Him I turn."*

I had the previlege of reading some chapters of this book to my respected father (may Allāh prolong his life) during his stay with me in London when he came for treatment. His guidance has indeed enriched this book.

I pray to the Almighty Allāh that He may accept this work with a good acceptance I am grateful to those who helped me in completing this book. I would like to especially thank his eminence the Grand Ayatullah as-Sayyid 'Ali al-Hussaini as-Seestāni (may Allāh prolong his blessed presence) who took upon himself the trouble to provide their answers to the questions. I am also grateful to the offices of the Grand Ayatullah in Najaf [Iraq], Qum [Iran], and London for helping me in ensuring the accuracy of what I have written and in ensuring that it is in accordance with the views of the Ayatullah.

"Our Lord! Do not punish us if we forget or make a mistake. Our Lord! Do not lay on us a burden as Thou did lay on those before us. Our Lord! Do not impose upon us that which we have not the strength to bear; and pardon us and grant us protection and have mercy on us. Thou are our Master, so help us against the unbelieving people."

'Abdul Hādi as-Sayyid Muhammad at-Taqi al-Hakim
27 Ramadhan 1418 / 26 January 1998

Glossary

Ahlul Kitāb:	People of the Book; that is, the Christian, the Jews and the Zoroastrians.
Al-hākim ash-shar'ī:	A mujtahid or someone authorized by him to deal in judicial matters.
Bāligh:	A male child of fifteen lunar years and a female child of nine lunar years.
Hadíth (**pl.** *ahādíth*):	Saying of the Prophet (s.a.w.) and the Imams (a.s.).
Halāl meat:	The meat from an animal that was slaughtered according to Islamic laws.
Halāl:	Permissible.
Harām:	Forbidden; not allowed.
Ihtiyāt wājib:	Precautionarily obligatory, obligatory based on precaution. (See wājib below.)
Ihtiyāt:	Studying the views of the most learned mujtahids and then adopting the precautionary line of action. For example, if some mujtahids say that deed 'x' is recommended while some others say that it is obligatory, then precaution demands that one must do it. Or if some mujtahids say that deed 'z' is disliked while some others say that it is forbidden, then precaution demands that one must refrain from it.
Istakhārah:	Literally, to seek what is good. It is a term used when a person takes a *tasbíh* or the Qur'ān, recites a prayer asking for Allāh's

help, and then moves a number of beads (in case of *tasbíh*) or opens a page from the Qur'ãn and reads the first ayat. Based on the number of beads or the content of the verse, one gets the indication whether he should or should not proceed with what he had intended to do.

Janãbat: The state of impurity caused by discharge of semen or sexual intercourse.

Kathír water: Any water is that is at least *kurr* in weight or flowing. So water from the tap or hose pipe is considered *kathír*. *Qalíl* means the water that is less than *kurr* and not flowing.

Kohl: Antimony a cosmetic item that is used to darken the edges of the eyelids.

Kurr: A body of water that is still (not moving) and weighs at least 377 k.g. or occupies at least 27 cubic span space. For example, a swimming pool, etc.

Libãsu 'sh-shuhra: Literally means "dress of fame," a dress is repulsive and ridiculous that invites people to insult and demean the person who wears it.

Mahram: A person who is related by blood or marriage and in whose presence the *hijãb* is not compulsory.

Marja': Literally, "the point of reference." It is a term used for the most learned mujtahid to whom the layman refers for guidance in *sharí'a* matters.

Mayta: An animal that died by itself or was killed without observing the Islamic rules of slaughtering. Whereas *zabíha* means an animal slaughtered according to the Islamic rules.

Muhajjaba: A girl or a lady with *hijãb*.

Mujtahid: The jurist, the expert of Islamic laws.

Mutanajjis: An item that has become *najis* by secondary reasons as opposed to *'ayn najis* (essentially impure).

Qalíl: A body of still water that is less than *kurr*.

Qiblah: The direction towards the holy Ka'bah in Mecca.

Sajdah:	There are four verses in the holy Qur'ān which are known as "verses of the wājib sajdah": 32:15, 41:37, 53:62, and 96:19. It is obligatory to do sajdah when one reads or hears any of these verses.
Tanāzul:	In principle, the money received for the meat that is not slaughtered according to Islam is not legitimate because that transaction is not valid. However, the rule of *tanāzul* means that you are withdrawing your right from that meat and accepting the money for the withdrawal and not for the meat.
Tawāf:	Going around the holy Ka'ba seven times.
Tawriya:	Making a statement that can be interpreted in two different ways: you mean one thing but you let the listener perceive something else.
Tayammum:	A substitute for wudhu (the minor ablution) and ghusl (the major ablution) when water is unavailable. It is done by striking the hands on the earth and then wiping the forehead and the hands. For details see the Manual of Islamic Laws.
Wājib kifā'i:	An obligation which is equally applied on all Muslims but lifted as soon as one of them fulfills it. On the other hand, if no one fulfills it, then all are accountable in the eyes of God.
Wājib:	Compulsory, or obligatory.

بســـم الله الرحمن الرحيم

الحمد لله رب العالمين و الصلاة و السلام على خير خلقه
محمد وآله الطيبين الطاهرين وبعد : يجوز العمل برسالة
(الفقه للمغتربين) والعامل بها مأجور ان شاء الله تعالى ·

ه رمضان المبارك

١٤١٨

In the name of Allāh, the Beneficent, the Merciful

All praise is due to Allāh, the Lord of the universe. May blessings and greetings be on the best of creatures, Muhammad, and his blessed and pure progeny.

It is permissible to act according to the book "al-Fiqh lil Mughtaribín," and one who acts on it will, God willing, be rewarded.

5 Ramadhān al-Mubārak, 1418
       'Ali al-Husayni as-Sistāni.

Introduction

On the morning of a sunny day in winter of Rajab 1416 A.H. (January 1995), the aircraft took off with me on board towards London, the capital of Britain.

When the aircraft moved from the east to the west, from the land of sunshine to the capital of fog, I could feel the warmth of the sun from the plane's windows, the warmth that I bade farewell to as I left my homeland.

When the plane levelled off at the centre of the sky and its flight become smooth and calm, as if it were firmly fixed on a central poll, I decided to use the time by reciting the chapters from the pocket-size holy Qur'ān that was with me. This has been my habit from my childhood since I set my eyes on my grandfather in our vast home in Najaf and heard him recite the Qur'ān every morning, afternoon, and at night, during his travells and at other times. And I also have retained in my memory the fact that my father used to carry a copy of the Holy Qur'ān in his pocket so that he is not far removed from it at home as well as away from home.

I opened the Holy Book and started reciting in a lowered voice the verses so as to purify my soul, to perfume my mouth from the dirt of matter and its temptation, and to seek the

Almighty Allāh's help protecting this flying object from the calamities of time.

It was midday, the time for noon prayer came close. I got up from my seat, went to the toilet, renewed my *wudhu* (minor ablution), and then I took out a comb from my pocket and combed my hair after the *wudhu.* Then I took out a small perfume bottle that I always carry in my pocket so that I may use it, for it is related that it is *mustahab* to use perfume, in that the Prophet Muhammad (s.a.w.) used to love it, and that a *salāt* with perfume is equal to seventy salāts.

After the *wudhu,* combing, and perfuming, I returned to my seat while I was still reciting some Qur'ānic verses that I had memorized from childhood.

Then I started thinking: Where will I say the salāt? How will I know the direction of the *qibla?* Is it obligatory to say the salāt in a standing position or can I do so while I am seated?

When these thoughts were going through my mind, I reclined on my religious knowledge and remembered that Islamic Jurists say: it is obligatory to say the *salāt* in a standing position as long as I can do so; if I am unable to perform it thus, I should pray in a sitting position. The format of prayer would move from one level to a lesser level based on my ability and the given ciramstances; but the obligation of *salāt* would not be waived from a Muslim under any circumstance.

So when I reached this conclusion, I looked around the plane to find a place in which I could say the salāt in a standing position. My eyes settled on a small area in one part of the plane that was sufficient for saying the salāt. I said to myself that the problem of the place has been resolved but now I have to find the direction of the *qibla* as long as the plane is flying in one direction. I decided to seek the help of the airline crew to determine the direction of *qiblah*.

An air steward passed for gathering the tea cups from the tables, I seized the opportunity and asked him in broken English as follows:

Can I ask you a question?

"Yes, go ahead."

Can you help me in showing me the direction of the *qiblah?*

"I am sorry, I didn't understand your question."

The direction of *qiblah*…the direction towards Holy Mecca?

"Are you a Muslim?"

Yes, and I would like to say my noon prayer.

"Let me ask in the cockpit and I will be back."

I realized that I should also have asked for something to put on the floor of the aircraft to pray on it.

When he came back with the answer on the *qiblah,* I requested him to bring me something like a blanket or a newspaper that I could place on the floor of the aircraft.

He brought a blanket which I spread on the floor and prayed noon and afternoon *salat,* two (rak'at) each as *qasr,* facing the *qiblah.* Then I recited the *tasbíh* of az-Zahrã' (a.s.) by saying *"Allãhu abkar"* 34 times, *"al-hamdu lil lãh"* 33 times, and *"subhãn Allãh"* 33 times. After the *tasbíh,* I thanked Allãh and returned to my seat while I was in a different and more content state of mind because I was afraid that saying the *salãt* in the plane would be difficult and I might be drawing unnecessary attention from the other passengers. But my fears were unfounded. It became clear to me that the *salãt* earned me a special respect and added esteem for me in the eyes of the non-Muslims, including the steward, who were on board the plane.

My thoughts were interrupted by the announcement that food will be served soon. The airhostesses started asking the passengers about their preference from the menu. One of them asked me if I would prefer fish or chicken. I asked for the fish not because fish is preferable to me than chicken but because I was not allowed to eat that chicken since I was not sure that it has been slaughtered in accordance with Islamic laws. This is a problem that I have faced many times in foreign countries.

Since I was born and brought up in a Muslim country, I have no lingering doubt regarding chicken, or fish bought in a Muslim market.

But in a Western country, the situation is completely different. And that is because I am not allowed to eat any meat until I am sure that it was slaughtered according to the laws of Islam. This normally creates hardship.

The meal was served to us and the tray that was placed in front of me contained the following: fish fried in sunflower oil garnished with fried potatoes, a little bit of rice, salad, a couple of green olives, grapes, black fig, dessert, water in a small container, and small packets of salt, sugar, pepper, two pieces of bread, a fork, two spoons, a knife, and a napkin.

I was really hungry.

I thanked Allāh first, then picked the fork and knife, and cut the fish into small pices that could be eaten easily…Right then, I stopped and the following thought passed through my mind: It is true that if the fish is of the type that has scales, and that it has come out of the water alive or died after being caught in the net, then it is permissible for me to eat it irrespective of the fact that the fisher man was a Muslim or a non-Muslim, and no matter whether the name of Allāh was invoked on it or not. This is correct. But the problem is the oil in which the fish had been fried. Was that oil ritually pure *(tāhir)?* And was the cook a Muslim?

These were the disturbing thoughts passing through my mind at that moment. So I stopped eating that fried piece of the fish, despite the fact that I was hungry! I put down the fork on the side of the plate and tried to recall the rules of these issues that I had read about in the Manual of Islamic Laws of my *marja'* when I was getting ready for the journey.

First I asked myself about the sunflower oil: is it ritually pure? I immediately responded in positive because the religious law says that "everything is pure for you until you come to know about its impurity." And since I did not know about the impurity of the sunflower oil, it was pure.

Now since the oil used in frying the fish was pure, the whole fish is pure, and thus I am allowed to eat it.

As for the cook who prepared the fish, was he a Muslim or from the Ahlul Kitāb (so he would be considered as *tāhir*) or was he a non-Muslim from the non-Ahlul Kitāb? This question is not important as long as I do not know that the person who fried it has touched it with his hand. And again the general rule of the *sharī'a,* "everything is pure for you until you come to know that it is impure", gave me a clear decision: the fish is pure, and I am allowed to eat it.

When I reached this conclusion, I breathed a sighed of relief. Then I picked up the fork and ate the fish. I looked at the fries for the same reasons and concluded that they were pure and ate them.

I did the same with the bread, salad, fruit and the dessert. I ate them all since they were pure. Then I drank the water and also the tea because they are also pure. This is what the religious laws tell me.

The plane was flying at 30,000 feet from sea level, and we still had two and a half hours before we reach London Heathrow International airport .

Inside the plane, some passengers were busy reading the morning papers, while others were in deep sleep. I stretched my arm and picked up a paper and started browsing through it.

My memory went back to the question that kept lingering in my mind for the last few days: "How will I preserve my religious identity from being destroyed in the foreign country?"

This has worried me for a long time since I thought of travelling to Europe, and it intensified the day I made that decision; at times I think about it and at other times it comes without thinking, leaving me only when I go to sleep at night.

I decided to meet a friend of mine who had been to London. My friend pointed out certain issues to me, and also took me to the bookstore and showed me a book that contained various issues that gave me a general idea of what I should do.

Both, the friend and the book, pointed out that I should place great importance on the following issue: "The negative elements of migration are not limited to the fact that it would not be possible to fulfill the Islamic laws by the immigrants or that they will not study the religion. The reality is even worse than that in the sense that migration would significantly affect the outlook of the Muslim, his habits, traditions, and also the state of his intellectual, moral and social aspects of life."[5]

The author of that book continues, "It is necessary for the Muslim who is compelled to migrate to a non-Muslim country to create by himself the religious climate that does not exist in those countries. Of course, he will not be able to create the

---

[5]   *Dalīlu 'l-Muslim fi Bilādi 'l-Ghurba,* p. 27.

general Islamic environment but he surely can bring about that atmosphere in a certain measure so that he may be able to arm himself with to the religious spirit that is suitable for him.

"Creating a suitable Islamic atmosphere is to some extent like inoculating against a disease from whose clutches one cannot escape—so he tries to deal with its danger by building a safety net around himself.

"Although we do not claim that this task is easy by any means, at the same time we cannot underestimate the great danger faced by a Muslim in his commitment to the religion which is the main foundation of his identity. So it is important to safeguard it even at the cost of loss in other aspects of life. Just as we emphasize the significance of these pitfalls, we must also emphasize safeguarding and protecting the Muslims from falling into them.

"A Muslim who struggles in those countries to secure his worldly future —in education or finance or other aspects— he is not supposed to lose his future in the Hereafter for the sake of this world. Just as a merchant is not allowed to lose his honour or life for the sake of material wealth, irrespective of its quantity, because it is worthless compared to his life and honour. Similarly, the sick person patiently bears the bitterness of medicine or the pain inflicted by the scalpel so that the disease may not spread and lead to death.

"So it is obligatory on a Muslim who resides in alien societies to protect himself against their adverse effects and dangers; and he must create an appropriate religious environment for himself that will compensate the loss of the environment that he had in his own country."[6] In this way, he, his wife and children, and even his brethren will be following the words of the Almighty: *"O you who believe! Save yourselves and your families from a fire whose fuel is men and*

---

[6]   Ibid, p. 36-37.

stones; over it are angels stern and strong, they do not disobey Allāh in what He commands them, and do as they are commanded." (66:6) They would also be acting in accordance with the statement of the Most Praised Lord *"And the believing men and the believing women, they are helpers of one another: they enjoin the good and forbid the evil."* (9:71) And also in accordance with what the Prophet (s.a.w.) said, "All of you are 'shepherds' and all of you are answerable in regard to your 'flock'." Thus would also be implementing the requirement of enjoining good and forbidding evil.

The spiritual immunization mentioned above can be achieved by the followings:

1. By committing to recitation of some chapters or noble verses from the Holy Qur'ān on a daily basis or listening to its recitation with humility, reflection and contemplation because in them are *"clear proofs from your Lord, a guidance and a mercy for a people who believe; and when the Qur'ān is recited, then listen toit and remain silent so that mercy may be shown to you."* (7:203-204) In words of Imam 'Ali (a.s.), "No one will sit besides the Qur'ān but that when he rises he will achieve an increase or a diminution: an increase in his guidance or elimination of his (spiritual) blindlness. You should also know that no one will need any thing after (guidance from) the Qur'ān and no one will be free from want before (guidance from) the Qur'ān. Therefore, seek it as cure for your ailments and seek its assistance in your distresses. It contains a cure for the biggest diseases, namely unbelief, hypocrisy, revolt and misguidance. Pray to Allāh through it and turn to Allāh with its love. Do not ask the people through it. There is nothing like it through which the people could turn to Allāh, the Sublime. Know that it is an interceder and its intercession will be accepted. For whoever the Qur'ān intercedes on the Day of Judgement, its intercession for him

would be accepted...">[7] It has also been said, "Whosoever recites the Qur'ān at a tender age, the Qur'ān will intertwine with his flesh and blood, and the Almighty Allāh shall place him among the respected and virtyous messengers; and the Qur'ān will be his protector on the Day of Judgement."[8]

There are certain copies of the Holy Qur'ān which contain brief commentaries that can be easily carried, and it will greatly benefit the Muslims in foreign countries.

2. Commitment to say the daily obligatory prayers on time, rather, even the recommended ones as much as possible.[9] It has been narrated that the Prophet Muhammad (s.a.w.) said to 'Abdullāh bin Rawāha in an advice to him when the latter was leaving for the Battle of Mu'ta: "You are going to the city in which there are few prostrations; therefore increase the prostrations."

Zayd ash-Shahhām narrates from Imam as-Sādiq (a.s.): "The most beloved of deeds with the Almighty Allāh is salāt; and that is the last advice of the prophets."[10]

Imam 'Ali has also advised us concerning the salāt: "Pledge yourself with prayer as much as possible and seek nearness (of Allāh) through it, because it is *upon the believers a timed ordinance* [4:103]. Have you not heard the reply of the people of Hell when they were asked, *'What has brought you into the Hell?' They shall say, 'We were not of those who offered the regular prayers.'* [74:42-43] Certainly, prayer sheds sins like the dropping of leaves (of trees), and removes them as ropes are removed from the necks of cattle. The Messenger of Allāh (peace and blessing of Allah be upon him and his progeny) likened it to a hot bath situated at the door of

---

[7]   *Nahju 'l-Balāgha* (ed. Subhi Sālih) p. 252 [sermon 176].
[8]   Al-Kulayni, *al-Usûl mina 'l-Kāfi*, vol. 2, p. 603.
[9]   See al-Hurr al-'Āmili, *Tafsîlu Wasā'ili 'sh-Shî'a*, vol. 4, p. 105.
[10]   Ibid, vol. 4, p. 38.

a person who bathes in it five times a day. Will then any dirt remain on him?"[11]

3. Reciting whatever is possible of supplication *(du'ã)*, wishpered prayers *(munãjãt)* and remembrance of Allãh, since they remind us of the sins, warn us to refrain from evil deeds, and encourage us to do good deeds. For example, the supplications in *as-Sahífah as-Sajjãdiyya* of Imam Zaynu 'l-'Ãbideen (a.s.), *du'ã* of Kumayl bin Ziyãd, and the *du'ãs* of the month of Ramadhãn like the *du'ã* of Abu Hamzah ath-Thumãli and the *du'a* of dawn, and the *du'as* of the weekdays, etc.[12]

This purification is needed for every Muslim, especially if he is in a non-Muslim country.

4. Frequently visiting the Islamic centers and organizations that observe the Eids, religious occasions, the birth anniversaries and death commemorations, as well as other religious programs like lecture and counselling — in the month of Ramadhãn or Muharram or Safar or during other months, days, and times.

In cities that do not yet have any dedicated center and organization, Muslims should observe the religious occasions in their homes. [Actually this is how early immigrants started to gather, and gradually formed a communities that later on rented or purchased a centre for their religious programs.]

5. Attending and participating in the Islamic seminars and conferences that are held in foreign lands.

6. Reading Islamic books, magazines, and newspapers for they contain both useful as well as entertaining materials.

---

[11] *Nahju 'l-Balãgha* (ed. Subhi Sãlih) p. 317 [sermon 199].

[12] Translator's Note: English translations of all these *du'as* are easily available in most centres in Europe and North America.

7. Listening to the various cassettes that contain Islamic talks that have been painstakingly prepared by the respected scholars and great speakers. In them you will find advice and counsel [for betterment of your faith].

8. Keeping away from the centers of entertainment and immorality including the viewing of immoral television programs and special channels that present movies which are not compitable with our beliefs, our religion, our values, our customs, our traditions, and our Islamic intellectual and civil heritage.

9. Establishing friendships with those who are good people for the sake of Allāh: you guide them and they guide you, you strengthen them and they strengthen you so that you may spend your free time with them in a useful manner.

In this way, you will stay away from those who are immoral in their behaviour, and also protect yourself from loneliness and its negative consequences. Imam as-Sādiq (a.s.) narrates through his forefathers that the Prophet (a.s.) said, "No Muslim person has gained a benefit after Islam [itself] better than a brother from whom he derives benefit for the sake of Allāh."[13] Maysarah narrates that Imam al-Bāqir (a.s.) said to him, "Do you have your own gatherings, talking and saying to one another whatever you like [i.e., without fear of government spies]?" I said, "Yes, by Allāh, we indeed get together, and talk and say whatever we want." He said, "I surely love your fragrance and your souls; you all are on the religion of Allāh and that of His angels. So help one another by piety and hardwork."[14]

---

[13] *Wasā'ilu 'sh-Shí'a,* vol. 12, p. 233.

[14] Al-Kulayni, *al-Usûl mina 'l-Kāfi,* vol. 2, p. 187; and also see the chapters on "visiting the brethren" (vol. 2, p. 175) and "remembering the brethren" (vol. 2, p. 186).

10. A Muslim should evaluate his deeds on a daily or weekly basis; if it there is good in it, then thank Allãh and add onto it; and if there is evil in it, then ask for forgiveness, repent, and make a commitment of not repeating it. Our noble Prophet Muhammad (s.a.w.) advised Abu Dharr saying, "O Abu Dharr, evaluate yourself before you will be evaluated, this will be easier for your appraisal tomorrow [on the Day of Judgement]; weigh yourself before you will be weighed; prepare for the great Judgement, the day when you will be judged. No secret is hidden from Allãh... O Abu Dharr, no person can be counted among the pious ones unless he be more critical of himself more than a business partner can evaluate his partner so that he may know the source of his drink and dress: has it been secured from a permissible or from forbidden [source]."[15] Imam al-Kãdhim (a.s.) said, "A person who does not evaluate himself every day is not one of us. If he has done good, he should ask Allãh to increase that; and if he has done an evil act, then he should ask Allãh's forgiveness and repent for it."[16]

11. Attaching importance to the Arabic language, the language of the Holy Qur'ãn and the language of numerous sources of Islamic laws and ethics. For those immigrants who come from Arabic speaking countries, Arabic is also the language of their ancestors: so they should encourage their children to speak it. Since the students in these countries learn more than one foreign language, it is better that they learn the language of the Qur'ãn so that they do not loose touch with their religion, heritage, values, history and civilization.

12. Attaching due importance to the up-aud-coming generation by bringing them —both males as well as

---

[15] At-Tusi, *Ãmãli,* vol. 2, section 19.
[16] An-Narãqi, *Jãmi'u 's-Sa'ãdãt,* vol. 3, p. 94.

females— up on the love for the Book of Allāh and its recitation by way of competitions and other encouraging activities. They should be trained to perform the devotional prayers and acquire good morals like truthfulness, courage, fulfilment of promise, and love for others. One should accompany them to the Islamic centers and organizations so that they get used to visiting those places. They should be made aware of the enemies of Islam, and the concept of Islamic brotherhood should be strengthened in them. They should be encouraged to participate in observance of various Islamic occasions and celebrations. In short, everything should be done to help them in better understanding of Islam and adopting the best manner of conduct according to its values and principles in this life.

The thought of how I should behave in the foreign country and preserve my individuality without being absorbed into another culture, and also without isolating myself and adopting the "seashell" attitude, kept haunting me. Then I asked myself: How will the others (among whom I shall soon be living) judge me?

My hometown [Najaf] which is filled with pilgrims and visitors the year round had conditioned me to judge the behaviour of a society by the behaviour of its members, or to judge a religion by the actions of its followers. If a visitor from a city would demonstrate good attitude, I would say that the inhabitants of that city are good people; and if a visitor demonstrates negative attitude, I would say that the inhabitant of that city are not good people, etc.

So it is natural that the people of the non-Muslim country where I shall reside will judge Islam through my behaviour as a Muslim and then generalize their judgement on all Muslims. So if I am truthful in my words and deeds, fulfill the promise, honour, the trust, abide by the general laws, help the needy, deal with my neighbour kindly, and follow the Prophet Muhammad (s.a.w.) example and respect his teachings, in that he has emphasized that "the religion [of Islam] is positive interaction [with people]" — if I do all this, then a non-Muslim who interacts with me will say: "Islam is the religion the higher moral ground."

But if I lie, not fulfill my promise, be abrasive with others, disobey the law of the land, harass my neighbour, cheat in my dealings, violate the trust, etc, then those who deal with me will say: "Islam is a religion that does not teach its followers high morals."

The pilot interrupted my thoughts and announced that we are flying over Germany. I opened my briefcase and took out a book that I had acquired to help me [in the foreign land]. Five *ahādíth* from Imam as-Sādiq (a.s.) in that book attracted my attention.

In the first one, addressing his followers, he said, "Be a source of pride for us, do not be disgrace to us. Make people love us and do not make them hate us [because of your behaviour]."

In the second hadíth, he quotes his father, Imam al-Bāqir (a.s.), "Be among those who are foremost in doing good; be thornless leaves. Those who have passed before you were as the example of thornless leaves, and I fear that you would become thorns with no leaves. Be those who call people to their Lord, bring them into the fold of Islam and do not make them abandon it. Those who were before you were recruiting others into Islam and were not making them abandon it."

In the third *hadíth*, after conveying his greeting to the faithful among his followers, Imam as-Sādiq (a.s.) says, "I enjoin you to fear Almighty Allãh, be pious, work hard for the sake of Allãh, be truthful in speech, trustworthy in handling trusts, prolong the prostration *(sajda)* and be good neighbour.

This is what Muhammad (s.a.w.) came with. Return things trusted to your custody, no matter they belong to a pious person or a sinner because the Messenger of Allāh (s.a.w.) used to enjoin the returning of even [small items like] a thread and a needle. Maintain relationship with your kinfolk, participate in their funerals, visit their sick, and fulfill their rights.

"If a person from among you is pious, truthful in speech, honours the trust, behaves well with the people, it will then be said that 'This person is a Ja'fari,' that pleases me and delights my heart because it would be said, 'This is the character of Ja'far.' "But if a person is otherwise, then his bad behaviour and disgrace is attributed to me and it is said, 'This is the character of Ja'far.'

"By Allāh, my father (a.s.) has narrated that if there is a Shi'a of 'Ali in a tribe, then he should be its pride: he should be the most trustworthy, the most deligent in upholding the rights, the most truthful in speech, and he should be one to whom people entrust their wills and trusts. When people inquire about him from his tribe, they would say, 'Who can be like him? He is the most trustworthy, and the most truthful of us in speech.'"

In the fourth hadíth, he says, "I call upon you to say the prayer in the mosques, to have good neighbourly attitude towards the people, to be willing to testify [for the sake of truth], and to participate in funerals — because you need the people; no one's life is independent of the people; people need one another."

In the fifth hadíth, the Imam (a.s.) answers the question of Mu'āwiya bin Wahab who had asked, "What should be our attitude between ourselves and our fellow tribesmen and acquaintances from the people who are not of our persuation (*madhhab*)?" He said, "You should look towards your Imams whom you follow and do what they used to do. By Allãh, they used to visit their sick, participate in their funerals, testify for and against them, and honour the trusts."[17]

Once I finished reading these ahãdíth, a sense of of relief overwhelmed me since they chartered for me the way I should act and outlined for me the code of conduct. At that moment, I made a resolution to compile in my notebook the most important problems that I shall face in the non-Muslim country and seek help from the books of jurisprudence that were in my briefcase. If I come across new problems that I cannot solve in the sources that are with me, then I shall write to the mujtahid so that he can answer my questions. With this I shall have solved my problems —related to ethics and jurisprudence— as well as those of the other immigrants.

This is how I started noting down my religious problems, one by one, and sought the expert opinion of the mujtahid on issues to which I have no answers in his Manual of Islamic Laws. Gradually this book came to existence.

This book is divided into two parts: Part One deals with Acts of Worship; and Part Two with Transactions. It also has three appendices.

Part One on the Acts of Worship consists of seven chapters that I think are more important to the immigrant Muslim than others. These chapters are as follows: Migration to non-Muslim Countries; *Taqlíd*: Following a Jurist; Ritual Purity and Impurity; *Salãt:* the Ritual Prayer; *Sawm:* Fasting; *Hajj:* the Pilgrimage to Mecca; and Death Related Issues. Each of these chapters begins with an introduction on the topic, followed by some rules that are relevant in non-Muslim

---

[17]   Al-Hurr al-'Ãmili, *Wasã'ilu 'sh-Shí'a*, vol. 12, p. 6ff. Also see al-Kulayni, *al-Usûl mina 'l-Kãfi*, vol. 2, p. 636.

countries, and ends with the most important question-answer [from the mujtahid] on that subject.

Part Two on Laws on the Mundane Aspects of Life consists of eleven chapters as follows: Eating and Drinking; Dress and Clothing; Dealing with Laws in Non-Muslim Countries; Work and Investment; Interaction in Social Life; Marriage; Women's Issues; Youths' Issues; Music, Singing and Dancing; and Miscellenous. Again each of these chapters begins with an introduction on the topic, followed by some rules that are relevant in non-Muslim countries, and ends with the most important question-answer on that subject.

The book also contains three appendices. Appendix I contains a sample of questions sent to the Ayatullāh as-Sistāni and his answers to them. Appendix II contains a list of main ingredients that are used in food items and which are forbidden to the Muslims. This is followed by Appendix III which has the names and pictures of the fish that have scales and are permissible for consumption.

At the end of the book, I have listed the references and a detailed table of contents.

* * *

'IBĀDĀT

LAWS ON
ACTS OF WORSHIP

* * * * * * * * * * *

* * * * * * * * * * * *

PART ONE

1. Migration to non-Muslim countries.
2. *Taqlíd*: Following a Jurist.
3. Ritual Purity and Impurity.
4. *Salãt*: Ritual Prayer.
5. *Sawm*: Fasting.
6. *Hajj*: the Pilgrimage to Mecca.
7. Death Related Issues.

Chapter One

MIGRATION TO NON-MUSLIM COUNTRIES

Introduction

A Muslim who is born and raised in a Muslim country where he consciously and subconsciously absorbs the laws, values and teachings of Islam, grows up into a young person who is aware of the customs of his religion, following its path and is led by its guidance. On the other hand, a Muslim who is born, and brought up in a non-Muslim country demonstrates the influence of that environment very clearly in his thoughts, ideas, behaviour, values, and etiquette unless his Lord helps him. This un-Islamic influence is seen more in the second generation of those who have migrated to non-Muslim countries.

This was the reason for Islam's view on ***at-ta'arrub ba'd al-hijra*** as reflected in many *ahādith*. *At-ta'arrub ba'd al-hijra* literally means "becoming shorn of one's percepts of faith after migrating [to city]," and technically, it means leaving an environment where you could follow Islam and moving to a place where you maybe prone to not following Islam. Such a migration is counted as one of the major sins. Abu Basír says that he heard Imam as-Sādiq (a.s.) saying: "The major sins are seven: killing a person intentionally; associating someone or something with the Almighty Allāh *(shirk)*; wrongfully accusing a married woman of adultery; Knowingly consuming usuary; running away from the battle-field in *jihād*; *at-ta'arrub ba'd al-hijra;* causing distress to only parents [by encroaching on their rights]; and wrongfully acquiring the property of the orphan." Then he said, *"At-ta'arrub* and *shirk* are one and the same [in severity]."[18]

Ibn Mahbûb narrates that some of our companions wrote through me a letter to Imam al-Hasan al-'Askari (a.s.) asking him concerning the major sins. He (a.s.) wrote: "The major sins are ones for which Allāh has threatened with the Hell-Fire; the one who refrains from them, He will forgive his sins if he is a believer. Those seven which cause [one to burn in Hell Fire] are: killing an innocent person; causing distress to the parents [by not upholding their rights]; dabbling in usury; *at-ta'arrub ba'd al-hijra;* wrongfully accusing a married woman of adultery; unlawfully confiscating the property of the orphan; and running away from the battle-field in *jihād*."[19]

Muhammad bin Muslim narrates from Imam as-Sādiq (a.s.): "The major sins are seven; intentionally killing a believer; wrongfully accusing a married woman of adultery; running away from the battle-field in *jihād; at-ta'arrub ba'd al-hijra;* unlawfully confiscating the property of the orphan; dabbling in usury; and every act for which [the punishment of] the Fire has been promised"[20]?

---

[18] Muhammad bin Ya'qûb al-Kulayni, *al-Usûl min al-Kāfi,* vol. 2, p. 281.
[19] Ibid, p. 277.
[20] Ibid.

'Ubaydullah bin Zurārah narrates that he asked Imam as-Sādiq (a.s.) about the major sins. The Imam said, "In the book of [Imam] 'Ali, they are seven: disbelieving in Allāh; killing a person; causing distress to one's parents; dabbling in usury; unlawfully confiscating the property of the orphan; running away from the battle-field in *jihād; at-ta'arrub ba'd al-hijra.*" Then he asked, "So these are the most major of sins?" The Imam replied, "Yes."[21]

Imam ar-Rida (a.s.) explained the prohibition of *at-ta'arrub ba'd al-hijra* as follows: "Since there is the danger that because of *at-ta'arrub,* he [the immigrant] might abandon [Islamic] knowledge, get involved with the ignorant people, and drift away"[22]

This, however, does not mean that entering non-Muslim countries is always forbidden. Other ahādith had described for us the reward of one who visits non-Muslim lands, the reward that every Muslim longs for. Hammād al-Sindi narrates that he asked Imam as-Sādiq (a.s.), "I visit the cities of polytheism [i.e., of the polytheists]; and there are some among us who say that 'if you die over there, you will be raised [in the Hereafter] along with them.'" The Imam asked me, "O Hammād, when you are over there do you talk about our affair [i.e., our truth] and call [people] to it?" I replied, "Yes." The Imam asked me, "When you are in these cities, the cities of Islam, do you talk about our affair and call [people] to it?" I replied, "No." The Imam said, "If you die over there [in the land of the non-Muslims], you will be raised as an *ummah* by yourself, and there will be light in front of you!"[23]

---

[21]   Ibid, p. 278.
[22]   Al-Hurr al-'Āmili, *Tafsílu Wasā'ili 'sh-Shí'a,* vol. 15, p. 100.
[23]   Ibid, vol. 16, p. 188.

General Rules

Based on these and other similar ahãdith, and other religious proofs, the jurists *(mujtahidín)* have issued the following rulings:

1. It is recommended for a believer **to travel to non-Muslim countries** for the purpose of spreading the religion [of Islam] and its teaching, provided that he can safeguard himself and his young children against the dangers of loss of the faith. The Prophet said to Imam 'Ali, "If Allãh guides a person from among His servants through you, then that is better than everything between the east and the west on which the sun shines."[24] When asked by a person for a counsel, he said, "I advise you not to associate anything with Allãh...and to call the people towards Islam. You should know that [the reward] for you for each person who answers [your call] is [equal to] emancipating a slave from the children of [Prophet] Ya'qûb."[25] (See the question-answer section below.)

2. A believer is allowed to travel to non-Muslim countries provided that he is sure or has confidence that the journey would not have a negative impact on his faith and the faith of those who are related to him.

3. Similarly, a believer is allowed **to reside in non-Muslim countries** provided that his residing there does not become a hurdle in fulfilling his religious obligations towards himself and his family presently as well as in future. (See the question-answer section below.)

4. It is harãm to travel to non-Muslim countries in the East or the West if that journey causes loss of the faith of a Muslim,

---

24   Ibid.
25   Ibid.

no matter whether the purpose of that journey is tourism, business, education, or residence of a temporary or permanent nature, etc. (See the question-answer section below.)

5. If the wife strongly feels or is sure that her travelling with the husband [to a non-Muslim country] will result in loss of faith, it is harãm for her to travel with him.

6. If the *bãligh*[26] boys or girls strongly feel that their journey [to the non-Muslim country] with their father or mother or friends will cause loss of faith, it is harãm for them to travel with the those people.

7. What do the jurists mean when they say **"loss of faith"**? It means either committing a forbidden act by indulging in minor or major sins like drinking intoxicant, adultery, eating forbidden meat, or drinking *najis* (impure) drinks, etc. It also means abandoning the fulfillment of a compulsory act like neglecting *salãt,* fasting, hajj and other obligations.

8. If circumstances force a Muslim to migrate to a non-Muslim country with the knowledge that the migration will cause loss of faith (e.g., a person seeks political **asylum in a non-Muslim country** in order to save his life), it is permissible for him to make that journey to the extent that it saves his life, and not more than that. (See the question-answer section below.)

9. If an immigrant Muslim residing in a non-Muslim country knows that his stay in that country will **lead to loss of faith** or of that of his children, it is wãjib on him to return to one of the Muslim countries. (See the questions at the end of this section.) As mentioned above, this loss of faith is realized by neglecting the obligatory acts or by committing sins.

---

[26] Translator's Note: *Bãligh* means the legal age in Islamic laws which for boys starts at fifteen lunar years and for girls at nine lunar years. Growth of pubic hair or sexual discharge is also a sign of attaining the age of maturity.

The obligation to return to a Muslim country applies only if it does not lead to death [for example, for a political opponent who has fled his own country] or does not place him in untenable situation or does not lead to an emergency situation where religious obligations are suspended (e.g., the necessity of preserving life which allows a person to eat harãm meat in order to prevent his own death from starvation).

10. If the journey is harãm for a person, then his journey will be considered "**a journey of sin**;" and, in such cases, he loses the benefit of the concession of praying *(qasr)* in four – rak'at *salãt* and also the benefit of not fasting during the month of Ramadhãn. As long as his journey maintains the status of "sin," he cannot benefit from such concessions provided by the *sharí'a* for travelers.

11. A son is not allowed **to disobey his parents** when they forbid him from travelling if their refusal to give permission is out of their concern for the son or if his journey will cause distress to them because of his separation from them — provided that he does not suffer loss by not travelling.

12. It is permissible **to approach the competent authorities** [like police and the justice system in a non-Muslim country] for various important issues —like prevention of harm befalling the person, the honour and the property of a Muslim— provided that is the only way for exacting one's right and preventing injustice.

Questions and Answers

Now we present some specific questions on the issue of migrating to a non-Muslim country and their answers by Ayatullah as-Sistani (may his guidance be prolonged).

13. **Question:** What is the **meaning of** *at-ta'arrub ba'd al-hijra* which is one of the major sins?

Answer: Some jurists have said that during our time, it applies to residing in countries that may cause the loss of faith. It means the migration of a person from a country —where it is possible for him to learn the obligatory religious teachings and laws, and where it is possible for him to fulfill his obligations and refrain from what is forbidden— to a country where this possibility does not exist fully or partially.

14. **Question:** A believer residing in Europe, America and other similar countries feels estranged from the religious environment in which he was born and raised. Neither does he hear the voice of the Qur'ān [recited from mosques] nor the sound of the *adhān*[27] coming [from the minarets]; and there are no holy shrines and their spiritual atmosphere that he can visit. Is leaving such an Islamic environment of his country and its positive aspects considered "**loss of faith**"?

Answer: This is not the loss of faith that would make residing in a non-Muslim country harām for that person. However, staying away from such a religious environment may, with passage of time, weaken the religious resolve of the immigrant to an extent that he may consider negligence of wājib deeds and committing of sins as insignificant. If a person has this fear that he might lose the faith in this manner, then it is not permissible for him to reside in that country.

15. **Question:** Sometimes a Muslim residing in Europe and America (and other similar places) indulges in harām activities that he would not have done if he remained in his Muslim country. The manifestations of temptation in non-Muslim societies may attract a Muslim to committing harām deeds even if he is not inclined towards them. Does this come under

---

[27]   Translator's Note: *Adhān* means the call for prayer announced at prayer times from the mosques.

the banner of the loss of faith that makes it harãm for him to stay in that country?

Answer: Yes; unless the sins he sometimes indulges in, and without insisting upon them, they are of the minor category.

16. Question: *At-ta'arrub ba'd al-hijra* has been described as "migrating to a country in which the religious knowledge of immigrant will decrease, thus becoming more alienated from his faith." Does this mean that a Muslim in such countries is duty bound **to be extra vigilant** so that lest he should become alienated from his faith?

Answer: The extra care becomes wãjib when not being mindful leads to loss of faith as described earlier.

17. Question: If a **religious preacher** who is mindful about his faith starts facing more situations where he commits harãm deeds because of the social environment (e.g., nudity and indecent exposures), is it harãm for him to stay in those countries; that is, should he stop propagation *(tabligh)* and return to his own country?

Answer: If he indulges in some minor sins occasionally, then it is not harãm for him to stay in that country provided he is confident that he would not be tempted to commit more serious sins.

18. Question: If an immigrant fears the **loss of faith for his children**, is it harãm for him to stay in that non-Muslim country?

Answer: Yes, the same rule applies to himself also.

19. Question: Is it wãjib on an immigrant in Europe and America (and other similar countries) to strive for **teaching** their children Arabic, and that ignorance of Arabic may lead in the future to ignorance of the main Islamic body of knowledge, and that will naturally lead to less familiarity with religious teachings and loss of faith?

Answer: To teach them Arabic is wājib only to the extent which is necessary for performing their religious duties that have to be done in Arabic (e.g., recitation of the Opening chapter of the Qur'ān, a second chapter, and other wājib recitations in *salāt*). Teaching more than that is not wājib as long as it is possible to provide them with religious knowledge in a foreign language.

Of course, it is recommended to teach them the holy Qur'ān [in Arabic]; rather it is important to teach them Arabic in a precise form so that they may benefit from the basic sources of Islamic teachings, especially, and foremost among them, after the holy Qur'ān, is the Prophetic *sunna* and the sayings of the Ahlul Bayt (peace be upon them all).

20. Question: If it is possible for a Muslim to reside in a Muslim country with some financial difficulty compared to his present situation, then is it wājib on him to travel to that Muslim country and leave residing in Western countries?

Answer: It is not wājib [to leave the Western country] except if he has no confidence in himself, in that he may lose his faith —as explained earlier— while residing in the foreign country.

21. Question: If a person has the ability **to propagate Islam** to non-Muslims or to disseminate religious knowledge among Muslims in non-Muslim countries without any danger of losing his own faith, is it wājib on such a person to do propagation *(tabligh)*?

Answer: Yes, it is *wājib kifā'i* upon him and all the others who have the ability to propagate.

22. Question: Is it permissible for a person to buy a passport [i.e., to **illegally obtain a passport**] or change the picture in the passport so that he may be able to enter a country, and then he would let the immigration officials of that country know the truth about his identity?

Answer: We do not allow it.

23. Question: Is it permissible for a person **to reside in non-Muslim countries** with all its temptations that confronts the person on the street, the school, the television and other media while he has the ability to migrate to a Muslim country although that transfer would cause difficulty in residence, loss of material wealth and comfort, and constrain the worldly aspects of his life? If it is not permissible to remain in such a country, would his efforts in propagation among the Muslims (reminding them of their obligations and encouraging them to refrain from harãm) change the rule for him and allow him to remain in that country?

Answer: It is not harãm to stay in that country if it does not create hurdles for him and his family in fulfilling their religious obligations presently as well as in future; otherwise, it would not be permissible even if he is engaged in some kind of propagation activities. And Allãh knows the best.

* * *

Chapter Two

TAQLÎD: FOLLOWING A JURIST

Introduction

Taqlíd means acting according to the opinion of the jurist *(mujtahid)* who has all the necessary qualification to be emulated. So you do what the *mujtahid*'s expert opinion says you should do, and abstain from what his expert opinion says you should abstain from without any research [in Islamic sources] on your part. It is as though you have placed the responsibility of your deeds squarely on his shoulders.

Among the conditions which must be found in a jurist *(mujtahid)* who can be followed is that he must be the most learned *(al-a'lam)* jurist of his time and the most capable in deriving the religious laws from the appropriate sources.

General Rules

Now it is appropriate to clarify the following issues:

24. A person who does not have the ability to extract and derive the religious laws must take up *taqlid* of the most learned mujtahid. The deeds of such a person without *taqlid* or *ihtiyāt* are null and void.

25. The most learned mujtahid *(al-a'lam)* is the most capable in deriving the religious laws from their sources.

26. In order to determine who is the most learned mujtahid, one must refer to the *ahlul khibra* (those who are sufficiently knowledgeable in Islamic jurisprudence). It is not permissible in this matter to refer to a person who has no expertise in this subject.

27. You can know the opinion *(fatwa)* of your *marja'* by one of the following three methods:

(a) By hearing the ruling from the mujtahid himself.

(b) By being informed about the mujtahid's *fatwa* by two just men or by a reliable person.

(c) By referring to the Manual of Islamic Laws *(risāla)* of the *marja'* or other books of that category.

28. When the *a'lam* mujtahid has no *fatwa* on an issue or if it is not possible for the layman to find the opinion of his *marja'* when he needs it, he can then refer to another mujtahid who is the second best in the line of hierarchy of being *a'lam*.

Questions and Answers

Now I present to the readers some of the questions on the issue of *taqlid* and their answers from Ayatullah as-Sistani:

29. Question: The jurists tell us that it is wãjib to emulate the most learned *(a'lam)* mujtahid, and when we ask the religious scholars in our area, "Who is the *a'lam?*" we do not get a clear-cut answer so that we may follow his fatwa. When we ask them about their answer, they say that they are not *ahlul khibra*[28] and they also say that: "we have asked *ahlul khibra* and have been informed that identifying the *a'lam* mujtahid requires the study of the books of the mujtahids and that obviously is a long and difficult task; so go and ask the others."

If the problem of identifying the *a'lam* mujtahid is so difficult in religious circles, obviously the problem would be even more difficult in other countries like Europe and America. After a lot of difficulty when we convince the youths of these countries that it is necessary to abide by the *shari'a* laws, we reach to the question of who is the *a'lam,* and find ourselves lost for the answer. Is there a solution to this problem?

Answer: If there are some *ahlul khibra* who refuse to identify the *a'lam* for one reason or another, there are other *ahlul khibra* who readily identify him. It is possible to contact those *ahlul khibra* through the religious scholars and others who are reliable and have contacts with religious seminaries and with the scholars in other countries. So although identifying the *a'lam* is not without difficulty, but it is not a serious problem.

---

[28]   Translator's Note: See rule no. 26 for meaning of *ahlul khibra.*

30. Question: How do we know who are *ahlul khibra* so that we may ask them about the *a'lam* mujtahid? How do we reach to them since we are far away from religious seminaries? Is there a way that can simplify for us the process of determining whom should we follow in *taqlid?*

Answer: The *ahlul khibra* are the mujtahids and those next in line in religious sciences, and they know quite well that one person in a limited group of mujtahids is the *a'lam*. And they have to consider the following three things to identify that *a'lam:*

First: His knowledge concerning the methods for providing the authenticity of the hadíth, and that involves *'ilmu 'r-rijāl* (the science of narrators of hadíth) and *'ilmu 'l-hadíth* (the science of hadíth). On this subject, issues like familiarity with the books [of hadíth] and the ahādíth that have been tampered with; knowledge of causes for fabrication [of ahādíth]; variance in the manuscripts and distinguishing the most correct one; and being aware of confusion which sometimes occurs between the text of a hadíth and the explanation of the compilers, are of utmost importance.

Second: His ability to understand the meaning of the text by considering the general rules of speech, specially the style used by the Imams of Ahlul Bayt (a.s.) in describing the laws. The science of *'usûlu 'l-fiqh* (Principles of Jurisprudence), Arabic grammar and literature, as well as familiarity with the views of the Sunni jurists who were contemporaries of the Imams play an important role in understanding of the hadíth texts.

Third: Soundness of his view in deriving the rules from the sources. And the method of getting acquainted with those in whom the status of *a'lam* is confined is by having scholarly discussions with them or by referring to their books or to the transcripts of their lectures on Jurisprudence and the Principles of Jurisprudence.

If a person cannot know the *ahlul khibra* by himself, he can come to know them through the religious scholars and others whom he trusts. The geographical distance should not be a barrier to establishing communication with them in this era where many fast means of communication are easily available.

31. **Question:** Sometimes the heart feels at ease in regard to a particular mujtahid. Is this feeling sufficient to do his *taqlid* if the *ahlul khibra* have difference of opinion in determining the *a'lam?*

Answer: If the *ahlul khibra* have difference of opinion in determining the *a'lam,* one must follow the view of those who are more qualified and capable among the *ahlul khibra*. This is the norm in dealing with all cases where the experts have difference of opinion.

32. **Question:** If the *ahlul khibra* have difference of opinion in determining the *a'lam* mujtahid or just say that following any one from the given number of mujtahids is sufficient, can a person apply the *fatwa* of one mujtahid in one issue and another mujtahid in another until it becomes clear for him who is the *a'lam?*

Answer: This question has three parts:

First: That some *ahlul khibra* announce that "it is sufficient to follow of one specific mujtahid or of a group of mujtahids." This has no religious value at all.

Second: That the *ahlul khibra* announce that two or more mujtahids are equal in knowledge and piety (in the sense of being careful in deriving the laws [from their sources]), then a lay person has the option of acting according to the views of any one of the mujtahids in **all** issues.

However, as a matter of precaution *(ihtiyāt)* in some issues, if possible, one could act in such a manner as to fulfill the requirements of both views; for example, in the case of praying concessionary *qasr* and full *(tamām)* prayers. [That is, pray the same prayer in *qasr* as well as in *tamām* forms.]

Third: That some *ahlul khibra* announce that mujtahid 'a' is the *a'lam* whereas others among the *ahlul khibra* announce that mujtahid 'b' is the *a'lam*. This can have two situations:

(i) A person knows that one of the two mujtahids is the *a'lam* but he does not know which one specifically. This is a very unusual situation and it has been discussed in detail in *Minhaju 's-Sāliheen,* question no. 9.

(ii) A person does not know which of the two is the *a'lam* in the sense that he thinks both are equal in knowledge. This refers back to the second of the three parts mentioned above, provided that the person is unable to identify the more Godfearing of the two mujtahids. If he is able to identify the more Godfearing of the two mujtahdis, he must follow the *taqlíd* of that mujtahid.

33. **Question:** If a person does not know the view of his *marja',* in a certain problem, is it necessary for him to find out about it even if it involves expensive telephone calls? Or is it sufficient to act on the known view of any other mujtahid until he finds out the view of his own *marja'?* And in such a case what will be the verdict on the past acts [done according to the view of the other mujtahid] if it differs from the view of his own *marja'?*

Answer: It is necessary for him to find out the view of his *a'lam marja'* even through telephone contact as long as it does not cause him harm [physically or financially]. If it is not possible for him to find out the view [of his own *marja'*], it is permissible for him to refer in that particular case to the other mujtahids, taking into account the hierarchy of the *al-a'lam* and the next *a'lam* in line. The deeds performed according to the view of the second mujtahid would be valid even if the worshipper later on finds out that it was not in accordance with the view of his own *marja'*.

* * *

Chapter Three

TAHÃRAT AND NAJÃSAT
RITUAL PURITY AND
IMPURITY

Introduction

A Muslim tries to maintain the ritual purity of his body, clothes and everyday commodities by avoiding contact with impure things because such contacts would render the other items impure and would necessitate the process of purification.

Residing in a non-Muslim country makes the process of maintaining purity difficult for some Muslims as they interact with its non-Muslim citizens in various situations of their day-to-day life: in restaurants, cafes, barber's shops, laundrettes, and, in public baths and utilities, etc. Therefore, it is appropriate for me to clarify for the respected readers the religious rules concerning *tahãrat* (ritual purity) and *najãsat* (ritual impurity).

General Rules

34. A well known religious law says: "Everything is ritually pure for you unless you come to know that it is ritually impure." This law declares everything to be pure unless one becomes sure a particular item has become impure. And as long as you are not sure that it has become ritually impure *(najis)*, it is to be considered pure and you can apply all the rules of purity to it without any hesitation or doubt.

35. The **Ahlul Kitāb** (that is, the Jews, the Christians and the Zoroastrians) are ritually pure *(tāhir)* as long as you do not know that they have become ritually impure *(najis)* by coming into contact with an impure object. You can follow this ruling when dealing with them.

36. The impurity **transfers from one item to another** through flowing wetness [that is, there is so much wetness in the impure item that it permeates to another item and makes it impure]. The impurity is neither transferred when it is dry, nor by non-flowing wetness. So if you place your hand on a dry *najis* item, your hand will not become impure.

37. You can **assume the ritual purity *(tahārat)* of any person** that you meet and shake hands with (even if that person's hand is wet) as long as you do not know his beliefs and religion — in such cases you can assume that he might be a Muslim or one of the Ahlul Kitāb. Moreover, it is not obligatory for you to ask him in order to ascertain his religion; that is, even if doing so does not put you or him in any inconvenience. (See the question-answer section below).

38. Any **water drops or other liquids** that fall upon your body or dress are to be considered pure as long as you do not know that they are *najis*.

39. All kinds of **alcohol** (whether extracted from wood or other sources) is pure, not *najis*. So the medicines, the perfumes, and the food containing alcohol are pure and can be used. It is also permissible to eat such food if the amount of alcohol is very minute, e.g., 2%.

40. No matter who was the previous user, the everyday **commodities and utensils** can be used without the need for purifying them as long as you do not know that they had become *najis* previously. (See the question-answer section below.)

41. If **the carpet and the mattress** become *najis* by the elements that do not have a mass (i.e., do not leave any marks or stains on the carpet or the mattress), it can be purified by sprinkling water over it from a kettle or a jug once until the pure water covers the impure area, and then wipe the water away by using a piece of cloth or a vacuum cleaner, etc. The carpet or the mattress will now be considered pure; and the water removed from it will be considered, on basis of obligatory precaution, as *najis*.

The same rule will apply in purifying the cloth if it becomes *najis* by impure sources other than urine. Things becoming najis by urine, will be discussed later on.

42. If one wants to purify the carpet or the mattress by using pure water connected to the *kurr* source [e.g., by using a hose pipe instead of pouring water from a jug], there is no need to wipe the water off using a piece of cloth or a vacuum cleaner, etc. As soon as the *kurr* water covers the najis area, it will become pure [and the water will also be considered as pure].

43. It is possible to purify the carpet or the mattress which has become *najis* by the elements that do have a mass (i.e., do leave marks or stains like blood or semen) by the same method as mentioned in no. 39 provided that the impure element is removed while washing or prior to washing. The only difference is that if it is purified by the *qalil* water [e.g., from a jug or a glass], then the water removed from the carpet will be considered *najis* as a confirmed opinion and not as an obligatory precaution.

44. If a carpet or a mattress becomes ***najis* by urine of an infant child** that mostly gets nutrition by breast-feeding, then it can be purified by sprinkling the water — even if it is just a little — on it until it covers the najis area. In this case, there is no need to remove the water by using a piece of cloth or vacuum cleaner, etc.

45. If a cloth becomes ***najis* by urine**, it can be purified by sprinkling little water on it from a kettle or a jug, etc., until it covers the *najis* area; then the water should be wiped off by using a piece of cloth, etc. You have to do this twice and then the cloth will be considered pure.

The water that has been wiped off from such a cloth (while purifying it two times) will be considered *najis* on the basis of obligatory precaution if there is no urine in it. Conversely the water will be considered *najis* as a confirmed opinion.

46. If one wants to purify such a cloth by pure water which is connected to a *kurr* source [e.g., under the water tap or by using a hose pipe], even then it is necessary to wash it twice. Similarly, it is necessary to wash the body twice —even when washed in *kurr* water— while purifying if it has become *najis* because of urine.

47. If the hand and the cloth become impure because of an intoxicating drink, a single wash can purify it. However, in case of purifying such a cloth in *qalil* water, it is necessary to rinse the cloth after washing.

48. Utensils and cups that have become impure because of intoxicating drink should be washed three times if purified by *qalil* water. If it is being purified by pure water connected to a *kurr* source, even then it should be washed three times, as a matter of obligatory precaution.

49. A single wash can purify the hand and the cloth that have become impure by **licking of a dog**. Such a cloth, needs to be rinsed if it is purified by *qalil* water. (See the question-answer section below.)

50. Utensils and cups that have become impure by licking of a dog or by the dog drinking from them can be purified as follows: first they should be cleaned by using earth or dust, and then by washing then twice with water.

Questions and Answers

Now I present to the readers some of the questions on the issue of *tahārat* and *najāsat,* and their answers:

51. Question: The earth is one of the purifying agents. Following the example of a shoe's sole that can be purified by walking on the earth, would the same rule apply to car tires?

Answer: The earth cannot purify the tires.

52. Question: Where does the domino effect of ***mutanajjis*** items stop when it is no longer wet?[29]

Answer: The first *mutanajjis* item would make the item that comes into contact with it impure; similarly, the second *mutanajjis* would make the item that comes into contact with it impure; but the third *mutanajjis* can no longer make other items impure no matter whether it is wet or dry.

53. Question: If a **dog licks** my body or clothes, how do I purify it?

---

[29] Translator's Note: An item which is impure by itself is known as *'ayn najis* or simply *najis*; the item that becomes impure by coming into wet contact with an *'ayn najis* is known as "*mutanajjis*," that is impure by secondary reason.

Answer: It is sufficient to wash it once. However, if the water is *qalil,* it is necessary to rid it of the water by wringing it.

54. Question: Are the **Sikhs** considered to be among the followers of the past revealed religions like the Jews and the Christians?

Answer: They are not counted among the People of the (Revealed) Books (the Ahlul Kitāb).

55. Question: Are the **Bhuddists** among the Ahlul Kitāb?

Answer: They are not from them.

56. Question: A Muslim who rents a fully **furnished house** in the West, can he considered everything in it to be pure as long as he does not find any trace of impure things in it, even if the previous occupant was from Ahlul Kitāb, i.e., a Christian or a Jew? What if the previous occupant was a Bhuddist or an atheist who does not believe in God and the prophets?

Answer: Yes, he can consider everything in the house ritually pure as long as he does not know that it has become impure. Just conjecture or doubt about impurity is of no value.

57. Question: The floor of most houses in the West is covered with **carpet** that has been glued to the floor in such a way that it is difficult to lift it off. How can such a carpet be rendered clean (*tahir*) if it becomes impure with urine or blood? The water used to purify in both the cases could be *qalil* or *kathir.* Please explain the ruling in both cases.

Answer: If it is possible to wipe the water off the carpet by using a piece of cloth or a vacuum cleaner, it can be purified with *qalil* water, provided that the water is wiped off the carpet, in the process. Conversely, it must be purified by *kathir* water [i.e., by using a hose pipe connected to the tap].

58. Question: In West, there are many public laundry places in which Muslims and non-Muslims wash their clothes.

Is it permissible for us to pray in the clothes washed in such facilities, especially we have no knowledge whether or not the washing machines are connected to the *kurr* water[30] at some stages of the washing, and whether or not it purifies the clothes in the process of washing?

Answer: There is no problem in praying in those **clothes that were pure** before washing them [in such facilities] as long as you are aware that they have become impure. [In other words, what goes in the public washing machine as pure comes out as pure unless you are sure that it has become impure.]

Similarly, [you can pray in] the **impure clothes** [that were washed in the public laundry machines] provided that you are reassured

[1] that the impure element, if any, has been washed away;

[2] and that the pure water covered the entire impure area twice (if it had become impure by urine and even if the water was connected to *kurr* source as an obligatory precaution) or just once (if it had become impure by other elements);

[3] and that the water was removed from the cloth by wringing or other similar method [i.e., spinning of the machine] if it was *qalil*.

However, if you are not sure and just have conjecture that the garment has been purified as per religious requirement, the previously impure garment will still be considered impure and praying in it would not be valid.

59. Question: Can the clothes washed with **liquid detergent** in laundry facilities owned by a non-Muslim be

---

[30] Translator's Note: All laundry machines are connected to *kurr* source because it comes from the main reservoir supplying the water to the city.

considered tahir while knowing that Muslims as well as non-Muslims wash their clothes there?

Answer: If you do not know that the clothes have come into contact with a source of najasah, you can consider them as tahir (pure).

60. Question: Some **soaps** contain pigs fat or other animals not slaughtered Islamically. Furthermore, we do not know whether or not chemical change has taken place in the manufacturing process. Can such soaps be considered tahir? [Chemical change is a purifying agent in the sense that it purifies a *najis* item.]

Answer: If it is proven to contain those [impure] elements, it is to be considered as impure except if the occurrence of chemical change is proven. Such a change is not proven in manufacturing of soaps.

61. Question: A **toothbrush** that contains bristles from the hair of a pig: is it permissible to buy, sell and use it? Does the mouth become impure by using such a toothbrush?

Answer: It is permissible to buy, sell and use it; however, the mouth will become impure by using it; and the mouth will become pure by taking that toothbrush out and getting rid of the remaining toothpaste from the mouth.

62. Question: If blood is seen in the yolk or the white part of the **egg**, does it make the egg impure and harãm for us? Is there a solution for it?

Answer: The blood inside the egg is pure, but it is harãm [for consumption]. Therefore, the egg can be eaten by removing the blood from it provided it is not very minute and been absorbed in it. [In the latter case, it is not removable and therefore the egg becomes harãm.]

63. Question: Are **alchoholic beverages** pure? Is **beer** pure?

Answer: There is no doubt about impurity of alchoholic drinks. As far as beer (*fuqā'*) is concerned, it is impure on the basis of precaution; however, there is no doubt in it being harām.

64. Question: The **people residing in Europe** are of different faiths, nationalities and religions; and when we buy moist or wet food items, the shopkeeper may touch it with his hands. Since we do not know his religion, can we consider that food as pure?

Answer: As long as it is not known that the hands of the shopkeeper were najis, the food is to be considered as tahir.

65. Question: What about the **leather** products made in a European country, if we are unaware of the source of that leather? It is said that some European countries import cheap leather from Muslim countries and then use it for manufacturing various products. Can we consider such leathers to be pure? Are we allowed to say salāt in them? Can such a weak probability [about it originating from a Muslim country] be given any credence?

Answer: If the probability of the leather originating from a *zabiha* (an animal slaughtered Islamically) source is so weak that normally people would not give any credence (for example, the probability of 2%), it is to be considered as impure and cannot be used in salāt.

But if the probability is not so weak, it can be considered pure and using it in salāt would be permissible.

* * *

Chapter Four

SALĀT:
RITUAL PRAYER

Introduction

The *salāt* has been described in some ahādíth as "the pillar of religion." Imam 'Ali (a.s.), after receiving fatal injury by Ibn Muljim (may Allāh curse him), in a part of his advice to his sons, al-Hasan and al-Husayn (a.s.) said, "[Feer] Allāh, and keep Allah in view in the matter of the salāt, for it is the pillar of your religion. [Feer] Allāh, and keep Allāh in the matter of the house of your Lord (i.e., mosque): do not leave it empty as long as you live."[31]

As-Sukuni narrates from Imam as-Sādiq (a.s.), "The Messenger of Allāh (s.a.w.) said, 'The Satan is frightened from a believer as long as he keeps up salāt on time; but when he starts neglecting them, Satan becomes emboldened and tempts him to major (sins).'"[32] Yazíd bin Khalifa said that he heard Imam as-Sādiq (a.s.) say, "When a person stands for salāt, mercy descends upon him from the heaven to the earth

---

[31] *Tafsílu Wasā'ili 'sh-Shí'a*, vol. 4, p. 35.
[32] Imam 'Ali, *Nahju 'l-Balāgha* (ed. Subhi as-Sālih), p. 422.

and the angels engulf him, and an angel calls out: 'if this person knew what is [the reward] for the salāt, he would never stop.'"[33]

From these [few selected ahādíth] we can understand the importance —clear, obvious and well-known— of salāt in Islam. And since salāt is like being in presence of the Almighty Allāh (as it has occurred in the ahādíth that a person standing for prayer is as if he is standing in audience of the Almighty), the worshiper should approach Allāh through his heart by not thinking or occupying his mind with anything worldly and its transitory aspects. The Almighty Allāh says in the Holy Qur'ān: *"Indeed successful are the believers who are humble in their prayers."* (24:1)

When Imam 'Ali Zaynu 'l-'Ãbideen (a.s.) said his salāt, he used to stand "as if he were a trunk of a tree: nothing moves on it except what is moved by the wind."[34] When the Imams, al-Bāqir and as-Sādiq (a.s.), stood for their salāt, "their colour would change to red and then yellow as if they were talking to someone whom they could see."[35]

---

[33] *Tafsílu Wasā'ili 'sh-Shí'a,* vol. 4, p. 28.

[34] Sayyid Muhammad Hādi al-Milāni, *Qādatunā: Kayfa Na'rifuhum,* vol. 6, p. 164 which has a special section on the prayers of Imam Zaynu 'l-'Ãbideen (a.s.).

[35] Sayyid as-Sistāni, *Minhāju 's-Sāliheen,* vol. 1, p. 193.

General Rules

66. The mujtahids say that **salāt cannot be skipped** under any circumstances. It means that it is not to be omitted whether one is travelling or at home; even if the time is running out, it is obligatory upon the Muslim, for example a traveler, to say his salāt in a plane or a ship or the car or a train whether stationary or moving; it could be performed any where: in the waiting room, in a public park, on the side of a road, or at the work-place, etc.

67. When it is not possible for the traveler to say the salāt in a plane or a car or a train in a standing position, he should say it **while he is seated**.

If it is not possible for him to find the direction of the *qiblah,* he should face the direction that he most probably thinks to be the *qiblah;* if he is unable to prefer one direction to the other, he should pray in whatever direction he is facing. If it is not possible to face the *qiblah* except for *takbíratul ihrãm* (the opening "Allahu akbar"), he should at the least say the *takbir* facing the direction of *qiblah.* (See the question-answer section below.)

68. It is permissible to ask the airhostess about the direction of the *qiblah* so that she may ask the pilot about it. If you have confidence in their information, you can rely on it even if they are non-Muslims.

Similarly, it is permissible to rely on scientific instruments for determining the direction of the *qiblah,* for example the compass, if a Muslim is convinced about its correctness.

69. If a Muslim cannot do *wudhu* (minor ritual ablution) for the salāt, then he should do *tayammum* instead of the *wudhu*.

70. The **length of day and night** differs from place to place. If the day and the night are clearly known by the rising of the sun and its setting, the Muslim should rely on the rising and the setting of the sun for determining the times for salāt and fasting even if that means that the prayers have to be said more frequently because, for example, the days are shorter or that fasting becomes lengthier because, for example, the nights are shorter.

71. In some place the sun does not set or does not rise at all for a number of days or months. As a matter of precaution Muslims should rely on the timings of the closest city that has night and day in a twenty-four hour period. Thus they will pray five salāts according to the times of that closest city with the intention of *qurbat* in general [i.e., without saying *adā* (prayer on time) or *qadhā* (prayer outside its time)].

72. If it is not possible for a Muslim to determine the beginning of true dawn *(fajr)* or the midday or sunset for his prayers and fasting, and he has faith in the timings given by the observatories, he can rely on same, even if the scientists running the observatories are non-Muslims—as long as you have faith in their determining true dawn or noon or sunset times.

73. For a **traveller**, it is obligatory to say salāt in *qasr* form; that is, he will recite the noon, afternoon and night prayers only two cycles *(rak'āt)* [instead of the normal four rak'āt] provided he travels for forty-four kilometers or more (in both ways), starting from the last houses of his city in normal cases.[36]

There are detailed and specific rules in the *Manual of Islamic Laws* explaining when to pray *qasr* and when not to pray *qasr* while travelling. (For some rules, see the questions-answers at the end of this section.)

---

[36] "In normal cases" means other than the major metropolitan cities where going from one end to another is considered travelling.

74. Praying **Friday** *salāt* with due attention to its required conditions is preferable to praying the noon salāt, and is sufficient; that is, if a person says Friday prayer, he does not have to say noon prayer.

75. Praying in congregation *(jamā'at)* is preferable to praying individually. Its preference is stronger in the dawn, sunset and night prayers. A noble hadíth says: "A salāt [in congregation] behind a learned scholar is like [praying] a thousand cycles; and behind a Qurayshi is like [praying] a hundred cycles." As the number of the worshippers increases, the preference [and the reward] also increases.

Questions and Answers

76. **Question:** A person used to make a mistake in the way he performed his *wudhu* (minor ablution) or *ghusl* (major ablution). After many years, he comes to realize his mistake while he has prayed observed, fast and performed pilgrimage during that time. When he inquires about his problem, he is told: "Repeat all your prayers and perform the pilgrimage again." Since saying all the prayers and doing the pilgrimage again is difficult, is there a solution which would salvage his prayers and pilgrimage performed with *wudhu* and *ghusl* that he thought was correct? Is there such a solution as a concession to this person so that he does not become disheartened and rebel totally against religious obligations in a society which encourages such kind of rebellion?

Answer: If he was ignorant out of innocence, and therefore did mistakes which do not harm in such cases (e.g., did not follow the proper sequence in washing the head and the other parts of the body in *ghusl;* or did wiping of the head or feet *[mash]* with a new water), then his *wudhu* and *ghusl* will be considered as correct; and, consequently, his past prayers and pilgrimage will also be considered correct.

But if he was ignorant out of negligence in learning the Islamic laws or did mistakes which do invalidate the act in general (e.g., leaving out some parts of the body which must be washed in *wudhu* or *ghusl*), there is no way to validate his past prayers and pilgrimage.

However, if there is the fear that he would totally rebel when asked to make up all the past prayers and pilgrimage, then it is not appropriate to ask him to do so. Maybe Allāh will improve his situation in future.

77. Question: Some people pray for years and even perform pilgrimage, yet they do not pay *khums*[37]. Is it obligatory on them to repeat their prayers and pilgrimage?

Answer: Based on precaution, it is obligatory on them to repeat prayers pilgrimage, if the particular dress that they used in prayers, in *tawāf* and in salāt of tawāf was from items on which *khums* had become due.

However, if only the dress they used in salāt of tawāf was from items on which khums had become due, and they were ignorant (even out of negligence) of the law or the status of the dress, their pilgrimage is valid, but they have to repeat salāt of tawāf if they had no excuse for their ignorance. [In this case,] they have, as a matter of precaution to return to Mecca [to perform the salāt of tawāf again], if it does not entail great difficulty; otherwise they can perform that salāt wherever they are.

Similarly, they will have to do the pilgrimage again if the animal offered as a sacrifice was bought with money on which

---

[37] Translator's Note: *Khums* is an annual Islamic tax applied, among other things, on the savings. See the *Manual of Islamic Laws* or the present translator's, *Khums: An Islamic Tax* for details.

khums had become due. However, if they had bought it with money whose unspecific portion was liable for *khums* —as is the case normally — there is no problem in their pilgrimage, even if they used it from the money on which *khums* had become liable; of course, they will be responsible for that amount [for payment of *khums*].

All this is applicable, if they knew about the obligation of *khums* and the law forbidding them to utilize items on which *khums* has become wajib or if they were ignorant out of negligence. But, if they were ignorant out of innocence, their prayers and pilgrimage are valid.

78. **Question:** If a traveller leaves his home town immediately after the *adhān* of noon prayer, i.e. without saying that prayer, and reaches his destination after sunset, has he committed a sin? And is it obligatory on him to make up for noon prayer?

Answer: Yes, he has committed a sin by neglecting the obligatory prayer in its appropriate time, and he has to make it up.

79. **Question:** Is the **ink** that had dried [on our hands, for example] a barrier to perform *wudhu* or *ghusl*?

Answer: If it does not form a mass that would prevent water from reaching the skin, the *wudhu* and *ghusl* is valid. However, if one has doubt whether it forms a mass or not, it must be removed.

80. **Question:** Is it permissible for a Muslim to involve in pleasure by continuing to watch an entertaining movie even, though salãt time is due, and then he goes to say his prayers just before it becomes overdue *(qadhã)*?

Answer: It is not appropriate for a Muslim to delay the saying of salãt from its preferred time (i.e., at the beginning of its time span) except for an excuse; what has been mentioned in the question is not an acceptable excuse.

81. **Question:** Is **cream** a barrier to water reaching the skin, and so it must be removed prior to *wudhu* and *ghusl*?

Answer: Apparently the effect left on the skin after it is applied is nothing but just moisture, and so it does not constitute a barrier to water reaching the skin.

82. **Question:** Some women let their **nails** grow longer than necessary for beauty. Sometimes a nail breaks up, requiring a cover that must be placed over the broken nail. Knowing that such a cover prevents water from reaching the nail in *wudhu* and *ghusl*, is it permissible to use it? How should *wudhu* and *ghusl* be performed with that cover?

Answer: *Wudhu* and *ghusl* with such a cover over the nail is not valid; therefore, it is necessary to remove it for ablutions. And the purpose mentioned above for the cover is not justifiable.

83. **Question:** When should one say his salāt full (tamam) and when should one say it *qasr* (two rakat instead of four)? Is the general perception about a person being resident of a city sufficient for him to say his salāt fully [in that city]?

Answer: The conditions for *qasr* in travelling have been mentioned in the *Manual of Islamic Laws.* When a person considers residing in a city for a long time, and in the general perception it is considered as such, he is not considered as a traveller (e.g., if he intends to reside in that city for one and a half year, it will be considered as his home-town after a month). But if he intends to stay in that city for a short while only and is considered, in the general sense, as a visitor, he should pray *qasr*.

84. **Question:** How can we know the **time of mid-night**? Does 12 p.m. mark the point of mid-night as it is commonly held by some people?

Answer: Midnight is halfway between sunset and true dawn. So if the sun sets at 7 p.m. and the true dawn begins at 4 a.m., then midnight will be at 11:30 p.m. The criteria for determining midnight are the timings of sunset and true dawn, which differ according to place and season.

85. Question: A person who believes that he will not be able to wake up for **dawn** prayer if he goes to sleep, is it obligatory on him to stay awake till the time of prayer? Is he committing a sin if he sleeps and does not wake up for dawn prayer?

Answer: It is possible for him to ask someone to wake him up for dawn prayer or use an alarm clock, etc, for this purpose. If these means of waking up are not possible, then he is not committing a sin by going to sleep unless it is considered, as is widely believed, an insult to and neglect of the salāt.

86. Question: How can we say our obligatory prayers in an **aircraft**, especially if we do not know the direction of the *qiblah* nor is the floor stable [because the plane is in motion]?

Answer: As for the *qiblah,* it is possible to identify its direction by asking the captain or the airhostesses because their answers usually carry validity and are a source of assurance. One should therefore act accordingly.

As for the stability of the floor where salāt is to be performed, that condition will be waived when it is not possible to achieve it. However, other conditions of prayers should, wherever possible, be observed. Under no circumstance should the prayer be delayed beyond its appropriate time span.

87. Question: How should we say our salāt in **trains and cars**? Is it necessary to do prostration *(sajda)* on something or is it not necessary, in that just bending of the neck would be sufficient?

Answer: It is obligatory to say salāt in the usual way where possible. So, one should face the *qiblah* in all stages of the salāt; if not, at least while saying the opening *takbir.*

Otherwise the condition of facing the *qiblah* will be dropped. Similarly, if it is possible to do the bowing *(ruku')* and prostration *(sajdah)* normally (e.g., in the aisle of the bus or the train), those parts of salāt should be done normally. But if it is not possible, then one should try to bow normally for *ruku'* and *sajdah* [for example, from a sitting position on the seat or the berth of the train].

For *sajdah,* one has to put the forehead on an item upon which *sajdah* is valid, even if by lifting that item to the forehead. If bowing normally is not possible, one should just indicate by bending the neck [halfway for *ruku* and fully for *sajdah*].

88. Question: It happens that the time for salāt has come while the student is still on his way to the university. When he reaches the university, he realizes that the time of salāt has ended. In this case, is it permissible for him to say salāt in the car although there are places in which he could pray, yet by going to those places he may risk becoming late [for his university]?

Answer: The delay in getting to the work place [or university] is not a good enough reason for praying in the car. This is because it involves not fulfilling some of its conditions while it is possible to get down and pray normally on the earth with all the conditions fulfilled. However, if the delay is going to cause him considerable harm or put him in an untenable situation, it is permissible for him to pray in the car, (without being able to fulfill some of prayer's conditions).

89. Question: It happens that the time of *salāt* sets in while the Muslim worker is **at his work-place**, — noting that finding work is not easy — thus, he finds it difficult to leave the work for salāt. Sometimes he ends up losing the job because of his insistence on saying salāt. Is he allowed to say his prayers as *qadhã*? Or must he say them [on time], even if it leads to him losing his job?

Answer: If the need to work at that place reaches the level of necessity, then he should pray in time in whatever way possible: even just by indicating [by lowering the neck halfway for *ruku'* and fully for *sajda*]. However, such a situation arises only exceptionally. So he should fear Almighty Allãh and not accept a job which leads to neglecting the pillar of faith; thus, he should remember the words of the Almighty: *"And whosoever fears Allãh, He will make a way out for him [from difficulties] and provide for him from where he does not expect."* (65:2)

90. Question: Many big companies and business in the West employ large numbers of employees who work in offices about whose ownership they have no idea. So what is the ruling on: (a) Praying in those offices and using the water for *wudhu?* (b) If praying there is problematic, what would become of past prayers said in those places?

Answer: (a) There is no problem in praying in those places nor in using the water for *wudhu* as long as it is not known to have been usurped. (b) If it becomes clear after saying the salãt that the property was usurped, the past prayers are valid.

91. Question: If I pray with a **leather belt** or a **wallet** made from leather of a *mayta* and realize it during the salãt or after finishing it but before the end of its time span or after the ending of its time span—what would become of that prayer?

Answer: The prayer with a wallet made from leather of a *mayta* is valid just as it is acceptable to pray with a belt made from such a leather, provided that the probability of it being from *zabiha* is not a very low probability that would be ignored by sensible people.

In the second case [of very low probability], if he was ignorant [of this rule] and realized during salāt, he should take it off immediately and his salāt would be valid.

The same rule would apply if he forgot [that he had the wallet or the belt on him] and remembered during salāt, provided that his forgetfulness was not a result of carelessness and indifference.

In other cases, he will have to repeat salāt in time or *qadha* as a matter of obligatory precaution.

92. Question: One of the famous trousers these days is the one known as **jeans**. It is made in non-Muslim countries. It has a piece of leather used as a label. It is not known whether the leather is that of an animal slaughtered Islamically or non-Islamically—is it permissible to say salāt with these trousers?

Answer: Yes, it is permissible.

93. Question: Is salāt valid if the person uses **cologne**? Is cologne ritually pure?

Answer: Yes, it is pure.

94. Question: Is it alright to do *sajdah* **on concrete** or on mosaic?

Answer: Yes, it is alright.

95. Question: Some prayer-mats are made of synthetic material; is it permissible to do *sajdah* on them?

Answer: *Sajdah* on such items is not good enough.

96. Question: Is it permissible to do *sajdah* on writing paper and on paper tissues, especially, it is not known whether or not the raw material it is made of was from items on which *sajdah* is valid?

Answer: It is not permissible to do *sajdah* on paper tissues, only after ascertaining that they have been made from items on which *sajdah* is allowed; it is permissible to do *sajdah* on paper if it is made from material on which *sajdah* is allowed or from cotton or flax.

97. Question: A reciter of the Holy Qur'ān recites a verse of *wājib sajdah*, on hearing it from a cassette player, is it obligatory on us to do sajdah in this case?

Answer: It is not obligatory.

* * *

Chapter Five

SAWM: FASTING

Introduction

The noble Prophet Muhammad (s.a.w.) gave an impressive sermon welcoming the month of Ramadhān. He said:

"O people! The month of Allāh with its blessings, mercy and forgiveness has come upon you. It is the most preferred of all the months with Allāh; its days are the best of days, its nights are the best of nights, and its hours are the best of hours. It is a month in which you have been invited as guests of Allāh and have been placed among those honoured by Allāh. Your breathing in it is [like] an act of praising [Allāh], your sleep in an act of worship; your good deeds are accepted, and your prayers answered. Therefore, ask Allāh with sincere intentions and pure hearts to help you in fasting and recitating His Book during this [month]. Indeed damned is he who is deprived of Allāh's forgiveness during this august month.

"O people! The gates of Paradise are wide open during this month; therefore, ask your Lord not to close them in your face and the gates of Hell-Fire are locked; therefore, ask your Lord not to open them for you. Satans are chained; therefore, ask your Lord not to unfetter them upon you.

"O people! Whosoever among you improves his character during this month, he shall have the pass [to cross] over the Bridge *(sirãt)* on the day when [people's] feet shall slip. Whosoever is lenient with his slaves during this month, Allãh will be lenient with him in the reckoning of his [deeds on the Day of Judgement]. Whosoever checks his evil deeds during this month, Allãh shall withhold His anger from him on the day he meets Him. Whosoever honours an orphan during this month, Allãh shall honour him on the day he meets Him. Whosoever maintains during this month, contact with his relations, Allãh will maintain His mercy for him on the day he meets Him. Whosoever recites a verse from the Qur'ãn during this month, his reward will be like one who has completed the recitation of the Qur'ãn during the other months."

Imam 'Ali (a.s.) said, "There are some who fast but will gain nothing from their fasting except thirst; and there are some who pray but will gain nothing from their prayer except tiredness."

Imam as-Sãdiq (a.s.) said, "When you fast, your ears, eyes, hair, skin, and all your limbs should also fast." He also said, "Fasting is not only [abstaining] from food and drink alone. When you fast, protect your tongue from lying; lower your eye-glances from what Allãh has forbidden [you to see]; do not fight with one another; do not be jealous of one another; do not backbite one another; do not abuse one another; and do not be unjust to one another. Refrain from false accusation, lying, fighting, suspicion, backbiting, and slandering. Be those who look forward to the hereafter, and wait for your days, waiting for what Allãh has promised for those who have prepared to meet Allãh. You must have tranquility, sobriety, humility, servility, and submissiveness of a slave who fears his master;

and be fearful [of Allāh's chastisement] as well as hopeful [in His forgiveness]."[38]

General Rules

It is appropriate now to explain some rules of fasting, and append to them the specific questions and answers concerning this important Islamic ritual.

98. Among the acts that invalidate fasting is intentionally **eating and drinking**. So, if a person who is fasting eats or drinks by mistake (e.g., he forgot that he was fasting) and not intentionally, his fasting is in order and there is no penalty upon him.

99. Among the acts that invalidate fasting of Ramdhān is intentionally staying in a state of *janābat* until the beginning of true dawn.

So if such a person intentionally remains in that state without performing major ablution *(ghusl)* until the beginning of the true dawn in the month of Ramadhan, then it is obligatory upon him to abstain from the forbidden things for the remaining of the day. (As a matter of obligatory precaution one should abstain with the intention of *"ma fidh dhimma* — what is expected of him".) They should also make up this fast some other day [after Ramadhan] with the intention of *"ma fidh dhimma"* and also incur the penalty, based on obligatory precaution.

If a person is sick and cannot perform *ghusl* because of his sickness, he should do *tayammum* before true dawn; thereafter, he will be considered to be in state of ritual purity. Thus, they will be able to fast.

---

[38]   For these and other similar ahādíth in the books of hadíth and in *Mafātihu 'l-Jinān* of 'Abbās al-Qummi, p. 235-237.

100. Among the acts that invalidate fasting in the month of Ramadhãn is for a woman to remain until true dawn in a state of vitual impurity caused by menstruation *(hayz)* or post-natal bleeding *(nifãs)* after it had stopped and while it was possible for her to do major ablution *(ghusl).* So if she stays without *ghusl* till the beginning of true dawn, her situation will be the same as that of the person in *janãbat* as mentioned above. If performing *ghusl* was not possible for her, she should take to *tayammum.*

101. It is preferable for the fasting person not to swallow **phlegm** that has reached the mouth, although it is permissible for him to swallow it. Similarly, it is permissible for him to swallow the **saliva** that has gathered in the mouth, even in large quantities.

102. Discharge of **semen** during daytime does not invalidate the fast; and the person should perform *ghusl* for *janãbat* for his salãt. So discharge of semen [during daytime] does not invalidate fasting.

103. Washing the teeth with **brush and toothpaste** does not invalidate the fast as long as the person does not swallow the saliva that has mixed with the toothpaste. However, the lingering flavour or taste of the paste that mixes with the saliva does not affect the fasting.

104. If a Muslim lives in a city that has daylight for six months and night for six months [e.g., the **northern part of Europe or Canada**], it is obligatory for him to move during the month of Ramadhãn to a city with 'normal' day and night so that he can start fasting, if not, he should move after that month to fast as *qadhã* (making up the missed fast).

However, if it is not possible for him to move, then he has to pay compensation *(fidya)* instead of fasting; that means giving 750 grams of food [rice or flour] to a poor person per day.

105. If a Muslim lives in a city where daylight in some seasons is for 23 hours and the night is only for a hour or vice versa, it is still obligatory for him to fast, if he has the ability to do so.

But if he is not able to fast, the obligation is forfieted. If it is possible for him to do *qadhā* later on [e.g., in other seasons or] by moving to another city, it is wājib for him to do the *qadhā*. If he is unable even to do the *qadhā*, it is obligatory on him to pay *fidya* in lieu of fasting.

Questions and Answers

- **106**. **Question:** Some people come to a city with the intention of residing therein for some years for a specific purpose [e.g., education] During this time, they do not leave their own home-towns for good. When the specific purpose is accomplished, they leave that city and go to wherever they like. How should they do their salāt and how should they fast [in that city]?

Answer: They shall pray fully; they can fast after having lived in that city for a month just as they do in their own home-towns.

107. **Question:** Is it permissible to rely on the European observatories [i.e., non-Muslim experts] for determining the timings of true dawn, sunrise, noon, and sunset for the whole year, including the month of Ramadhān, knowing well that it is scientific and very precise to the minutes and seconds?

Answer: If one is sure of the correctness of their timings, it is permissible to act upon it. However, one should know that there are some differences in determining the true dawn specially in some of the cities in [northern] Europe [and Canada]; therefore, it is necessary to ascertain that it is based on the proper view.

108. Question: In some cities, the sun does not rise at all for days or does not set at all for days or even more. How should we pray and fast?

Answer: As for salāt, one should, as a matter of obligatory precaution, observe the closest place that has night and day in a twenty-four hour period, then say salāt according to its timings with the intention of *mutlaqa* [i.e., just *qurbatan ilal lah* without specifying whether it is *ada* (on time) or *qadhā* (after time)].

As for fasting, it is obligatory upon you to move during the month of Ramadhān to another city where you can observe fasting of this holy month, or move to that city after that month to perform it *qadhā*.

109. Question: Can a person who is fasting in the holy month of Ramadhān serve food to non-Muslims?

Answer: By looking at the issue on its own merit, there is no problem in it.

110. Question: Would use of a **nozzle spray** that facilitates breathing invalidate the fast?

Answer: If the spray that comes out of the nozzle enters the respiratory tract and not the passage of food and drink, it does not invalidate fast.

111. Question: Does the nutrition given, **intravenously** invalidate fast irrespective of whether or not it was absolutely necessary for the patient?

Answer: In both the cases, it does not invalidate the fasting.

112. Question: Does **masturbating** during daytime of Ramadhān invalidate the fast, regardless of whether or not it leads to ejaculation? What is the penalty that should be incurred by one who does so? What is the ruling for a woman who engages in masturbation during daytime of Ramadhān, irrespective of whether or not it leads to discharge?

Answer: If a person masturbates with the intention of ejaculating and actually ejaculates, his fast is rendered invalid and he must make it up by way of *qadhã* as well as pay the penalty *(kaffãra)* which is fasting for two successive months or feeding sixty poor people.

If he masturbates with the intention of ejaculating but does not ejaculate, he must complete the fast with the intention of pleasing the Almighty and then do it *qadhã*.

If he masturbates without the intention of ejaculating and he does not normally ejaculate, knowing that discharge is probable and it actually happens —he has to do *qadhã* without the penalty. However, if such a person was confident that no discharge would take place and it actually happens — no *qadhã* is required.

In all these cases, there is no difference between a man and a woman.

113. Question: A believer fasts but does not know that intentionally getting into **state of *janãbat*** invalidates fasting— what should he do [when he finds outs]?

Answer: It is obligatory him to make up those fasts; however, there is no penalty on him as long as he was [erroneously] convinced that being in a state of *janãbat* does not invalidate fast or was unaware of that ruling.

114. Question: According to some jurists, a person who intentionally invalidates his fast during the month of Ramadhãn by committing a sin has to pay the **all three kinds** of penalty [that is, fasting for sixty days, feeding sixty people, and emancipating a slave]. What should a person therefor do during our time when emancipating a slave is impossible since there are no slaves?

Answer: The penalty of emancipating a slave is waived when it is no more possible. It should be howeverclarified that in our view, it is not obligatory to pay the all three kinds of penalty for invalidating a fast during Ramadhãn by committing a sin. And Allãh knows the best.

115. Question: If the **new moon** is sighted in the East, does it apply to us also in the West? And if it is sighted in America, does it apply to Europe also?

Answer: If the new moon is sighted in the East, it also applies to the West as long as the latitude of the two locations are not greatly further away from one another.

If the new moon is sighted in the West, it does not apply to the East unless it is proven—even by the moon staying on the first [Western] horizon for the length of time that is longer than the difference between the sunset of the two locations. [For example, if the sunset in the Eastern city was half an hour before the Western city where the moon was sighted, and the moon stays on the horizon longer than half an hour —the Eastern city can follow the moon sighted in the Western city.]

* * *

In *Minhãju 's-Sãliheen,* it says: "The new moon is proven through the knowledge acquired by sighting or recurring reports etc., and through credible reports of its sighting, etc."

In ruling no. 1044, it says: "If the new moon is sighted in a city, it is sufficient for other cities, provided they share the horizon, in the sense that the actual sighting in the first city would necessarily be followed with the sighting in the second city if there were no barriers like clouds, fog, mountains, etc."

In the light of what has been quoted, the following questions arise:

116. Question: Would the sighting of the new moon in cities in the East like Iran, Ahsã', Qatíf [both in Arabia], other countries in the Gulf, Iraq, Syria, and Lebanon necessarily be followed by its sighting in Western countries like England,

France and Germany if there were no barriers like clouds and fog?

Answer: Yes, the sighting of the new moon in an area would necessarily be followed —provided there were no barriers— in places which are located to its west as long as they are not far apart on the latitude lines.

117. Question: If the answer to the previous question is positive, would the occurrence of the sighting of the new moon in views of some religious scholars in Eastern countries be a sufficient evidence for one who is residing in Western countries even though the sighting of the new moon did not occur in those places for lack of clear kies?

Answer: It will not be a sufficient evidence for him or for others. However, if the occurrence of the sighting from the view point of those religious scholars attracts trustworthiness in that person that the moon was actually sighted or proof was established about the sighting without any counter proof — even in the form of a ruling— that person can act on what he believes is true.

118. Question: During certain months, it is declared that the sighting has been proven according to some religious scholars in some Eastern countries. This is based on the testemony of those who have sighted the new moon. Such declarations are usually coupled with the following facts:

(a) The witnesses who sighted the moon and who number around thirty, for example, are scattered in various cities such as 2 in Isfahan, 3 in Qum, 2 in Yazd, 4 in Kuwait, 5 in Bahrain, 2 in Ahsã', and 6 in Syria, etc.

(b) The sky was clear in a number of cities in the West, and the believers went out in the attempt to sight the moon; and there was nothing preventing the sighting.

(c) The observatories in England announced that it was impossible to sight the new moon that evening in England except by using a telescope; and that its sighting with the naked eye would be possible only in the following night.

So, what is the ruling in such a case? Please guide us, may Allāh reward you.

Answer: The criterion is the satisfaction of the individual himself [1] about the actual sighting [of the new moon] or [2] the proof of sighting without any counter claim.

In the case mentioned above, satisfaction is not normally achieved concerning the appearance of the new moon on the horizon in such a way that it could have been sighted by the naked eye. On the contrary, one is satisfied that it was not sighted and that the testimony [of sightings in the Eastern cities] is based on illusion and error in sight. And Allāh knows the best.

* * *

Chapter Six

HAJJ: PILGRIMAGE TO MECCA

Introduction

The pilgrimage to Mecca *(hajj)* is one of the common obligations in Islamic laws. The holy Qur'ān has clearly mentioned this obligation. Almighty Allāh says in His holy Book: *"And it is for the sake of Allāh [a duty] upon the people to do the pilgrimage of the House—whosoever has the ability [to travel] to it. And whosoever is ungrateful, then surely Allāh is free from need of the universe."* (2:196) The Almighty has compared the negligence of *hajj* to ingratitude because of its importance.

Hajj is one of the five pillars on which Islam is based. In a noble hadíth, Imam al-Bāqir (a.s.) said, "Islam is based on five pillars: on prayer *(salāt)*, alms *(zakāt)*, pilgrimage *(hajj)*, fasting *(sawm),* and devotion [to the Ahlul Bayt] *(wilāya)*."[39]

Imam 'Ali bin Abi Tālib (a.s.) advised about hajj by saying, "Do not neglect the pilgrimage to the House of your

---

[39]   *Tafsílu Wasā'ili 'sh-Shí'a,* vol. 1, p. 20.

Lord otherwise you will perish."[40] Imam as-Sādiq (a.s.) said, "If the people neglect the pilgrimage to this House, the chastisement will overwhelm them and they would not be warned [about it]."[41] This is so because neglecting hajj while the person is in a position to fulfill all its conditions is a great sin. A hadíth says, "When a person is capable of doing the pilgrimage but does not do it, he has indeed flouted a law from the laws of Islam."[42] Another noble hadíth says, "One who keeps postponing hajj until he dies, Allāh will resurrect him on the Day of Judgement as a Jew or a Christian."[43]

General Rules

It seems appropriate now to clarify some rules about hajj.

119. When a Muslim becomes capable, hajj becomes obligatory upon him. By "**capability**" we mean the following:

(a) Availability of enough time to travel to the holy places and stay there for performing the obligatory rites.

(b) Physical health and strength observing to travel to the holy places, and stay there for the obligatory rituals.

(c) The road through which one has to pass for performing the rituals be open and secure in the sense that it does not place the life or property or honour of the pilgrim in undue danger.

(d) Financial ability: One should be able to get whatever is necessary for the pilgrim in his journey; e.g., food, drink,

---

[40] Ibid, vol. 11, p. 23.
[41] Ibid, p. 22.
[42] Ibid, p. 28.
[43] Shaykh as-Sadûq, Muhammad bin 'Ali Ibn Bābwayh, *Man La Yahdhuruhu 'l-Faqih,* vol. 4, p. 266.

clothes, including the means of transportation according to his status by which he can cover the distance for hajj.

(e) The financial position of the person should be such that by travelling for hajj or by spending from his wealth for the pilgrimage, he would not be putting himself and his dependents in need and poverty.

120. Hajj Tamattu': This is a kind of pilgrimage that is obligatory upon those who live in other countries i.e. far away from Mecca. Hajj Tamattu' consists of two rituals: the first is known as *'umrah,* and the second *hajj.*

121. In *'umrah,* five things are obligatory:

(a) Putting on the pilgrim's dress *(ihrām)* from one of the *miqāts. Mawāqít* (plural of *miqāt*) are locations [around the holy territory of Mecca] that *sharí'a* has specifically fixed for putting on the *ihrām.*

(b) Circumambulating *(tawāf)* around the Ka'ba seven times.

(c) The salāt of tawāf.

(d) *Sa'i* (i.e., brisk walking) between the hills of Safa and Marwa seven times.

(e) *Taqsír:* cutting off a little bit of your hair or cutting the nail.

122. The obligatory acts of *hajj tamattu'* are thirteen as follows:

(a) Putting on the *ihrām* from Mecca.

(b) Staying in 'Arafāt on the 9th of Dhu 'l-Hijja.

(c) Staying a part of the night (eve of 10th Dhu 'l-Hijja) until sunrise in Muzdalifa.

(d) Stoning the smaller pillar in Mina on the day of 'Eid (i.e., 10th of Dhu 'l-Hijja).

(e) Sacrificing an animal in Mina on the day of 'Eid or during the days of *tashríq* [i.e., 11th to 13th of Dhu 'l-Hijja].

(f) Shaving one's head or doing *taqsír* in Mina. By doing this, the pilgrim is free from the restrictions of *ihrām,* except the use of perfume and sexual contact with women. Based on obligatory precaution, the restriction of hunting continues even after shaving or *taqsír.*

(g) Tawāf of Ziyārat seven times after returning to Mecca.

(h) Salāt of Tawāf.

(i) *Sa'i* between Safa and Marwa seven times. With this, the restriction of using perfume is also lifted.

(j) Tawāf of Nisā' seven times.

(k) Salāt of Tawāt of Nisā'. With this, sexual contact with women becomes permissible.

(l) Staying during the night in Mina on the eve of 11th and 12th Dhu 'l-hijja. And also, under some circumstance, the eve of 13th Dhu 'l-hijja.

(m) Stoning the three pillars in Mina on the 11th and the 12th of Dhu 'l-hijja. And also, under some circumstance, on the day of 13th Dhu 'l-hijja.

Questions and Answers

123. Question: Is it permissible to put on the **ihrām** for hajj **from** the city of **Jeddah**? If it is not permissible, what should one do since the plane lands in Jeddah?

Answer: Jeddah is neither a *miqāt* nor parallel to any of the *miqāts;* therefore, it is not in order to put on the *ihrām* from there for 'umrah or hajj. However, if one knows that between Jeddah and the Haram [the holy territory around Mecca], there is a place which is parallel to one of the *miqāts* —this is not improbable if one looks for a parallel of Juhfah— he can put on the *ihrām* from there by offering *nadhr.* [*Nadhr* means making a vow in the name of Allāh that he will put on the *ihram* from place x.]

124. Question: While shaving the head in Mina, if the pilgrim's head is injured and blood flows out, what should he do in that case? And what are the implications [as far as penalty is concerned]?

Answer: If the injury was not intentional, there is nothing upon him.

125. Question: It is recommended to perform hajj every year. However, there are many poor Muslims who are in dire need of food and clothing in various Muslim countries. If it comes to making a choice between spending the money for hajj repeatedly or ziyārat (pilgrimage to the shrine of one of the Infallibles [a.s.]) and between giving in charity for those believers—which is more meritorious?

Answer: In principle, helping those needy Muslims is better than a recommended hajj or ziyārat of the holy shrines. However, at times the hajj or the ziyārat is associated with certain other issues that can elevate them to the same or even higher status of virtue.

126. Question: The Kingdom of Saudi Arabia assigns the places for pilgrims in 'Arafāt and Mina. We do not know whether or not those appointed places are within the boundaries required by the *shari'a?* Are we obliged to inquire and ask about the matter?

Answer: If it is within the known boundaries and the signs that are normally known for religious rites from generation to generation, it is not necessary to inquire about it.

127. Question: It has been said that some parts or the entire area of slaughtering in Mina is outside the boundary. Is it therefore obligatory upon us to ascertains the fact before the slaughtering? Knowing that ascertaining about one area and then going towards the other and again ascertaining about it is a difficult task, especially on the day of Eid, as you yourself know, where the time is also a factor. So what is the solution?

Answer: It is obligatory to ascertain in order to do the slaughtering inside Mina. If it is not possible because of overcrowding in Mina, it is permissible to do it in the valley of Muhassar. Moreover, the timing of slaughtering is not restricted to the day of Eid; it can be done till the last day of the days of *tashríq* [i.e., till the 13th of Dhu 'l-Hijja].

128. Question: Pilgrims are faced with one more problem regarding slaughtering, which represents more of a mental anguish: the animals slaughtered [in Mina] are wasted in spite of the fact that there are many poor people amongst us spread all over the Muslim countries who go without tasting meat for days! So is it acceptable for us to do the slaughtering in our own cities; or is there a religious solution that you can suggest for the people?

Answer: It is necessary to fulfill the religious duty by doing the slaughtering in Mina. As for the sin of wasting the meat of the animals slaughtered, if it actually happens, it is on the shoulders of the authorities in charge.

129. Question: If the exam schedule for a student conflicts with the timing of the hajj, is it permissible for him to postpone the hajj that year especially if the exam was very important for him?

Answer: If he is sure that he will be able to perform hajj in the following year, it is permissible for him to postpone it; otherwise, it is not permissible. However, if postponing the exam will cause difficulty to such an extent that it is normally unbearable, it is not obligatory on him to perform hajj that year.

130. Question: A person on whom hajj had become obligatory but he has not yet fulfilled it—is such a person allowed to go for *'umrah* in the month of Rajab? What if hajj became obligatory on him in Ramadhān, can he go for *'umrah* [before performing hajj]?

Answer: The *'umrah mufrada* (minor pilgrimage done off-season) is permissible for him. However, if going to *'umrah* would financially prevent him from going for hajj, then it is not permissible for him to do *'umrah*.

131. Question: A single young man has become capable to perform hajj; he is also thinking about marriage. Now if he goes for hajj, his marriage ceremony will be delayed for a while. Which of the two is preferable [marriage or pilgrimage]?

Answer: He should perform the hajj and postpone the marriage unless postponing the marriage entails difficulty to the extent that it is normally unbearable. And Allah knows the best.

* * *

Chapter Seven

DEATH RELATED ISSUES

Introduction

Almighty Allāh says in the Qur'ān: *"Every person is going to taste death, and you shall only be paid fully your reward on the resurrection day; then whoever is removed far away from the fire and is made to enter the garden, he indeed has attained the object; and the life of this world is nothing but a provision of vanities."* (3:185) He also said, *"And no one knows what he shall earn on the morrow; and no one knows in what land he shall die; surely Allāh is Knowing, Aware."* (31:34)

General Rules

Here are some rules in brief concerning the dying person, washing of the corpse and its shrouding, and burial procedure.[44]

[Before Death]

132. It's a matter of obligatory precaution one should move the dying person in the direction of the *qiblah* during the last moments of his life. This is to be done by placing him on his back with his feet pointing towards the *qiblah* as though if he sits up, his face would be facing in that direction.

It is recommended to read and ask the dying person to repeat the testament of belief *(shahāda)* concerning the Oneness of God and the faith in Prophet Muhammad (s.a.w.) and the Imams (a.s.).

133. It is recommended to close the eyes of the dead person, their mouth, stretch their arms along their sides, straighten their legs, cover the body with a sheet of cloth, recite the Qur'ān, and light up the room in which they lived.

It is disliked to leave the corpse alone.

[Ablution (Ghusl) for the Corpse]

134. After getting rid of the impure *(najis)* elements that are on the body of the dead person (e.g., blood, semen, etc.), the corpse has to be given three ablutions as follows:

(a) First wash it with *sidr* water. That is, water to which a little of *sidr* has been added.[45]

(b) Second wash with camphour water. That is, water to which a little bit of camphour has been added.

---

[44] For further details, see Sayyid as-Sistāni, *Minhāju 's-Sāliheen,* vol. 1, p. 95 ff.; as-Sistāni, *al-Masā'ilu 'l-Muntakhaba,* p. 50 ff.

[45] Translator's Note: *Sidr* is name of a lotus tree; "*sidr* water" means the water to which *sidr* leaves have been added.

(c) Third wash with pure water.

If *sidr* is not available, then it is precautionarily obligatory to wash the corpse with pure water instead. Similarly, if camphour is not available, it is precautionarily obligatory to wash it with pure water instead. Then it should be washed the third time with pure water. In such a case, after the three washings, one *tayammum* should be performed on the corpse.

135. It is necessary that the ablution given to the corpse be of the *tartibi* kind: that is, the body should be washed in **proper sequence** with the head and the neck first, then the right side of the body, and then the left side.

136. The person washing the corpse must be of the same **gender** as the dead person. So a male should wash a male corpse, and a female should wash the female corpse.

However, husband and wife are allowed to perform ablution to one another; although it is better that the washing be done with the body covered with a sheet of cloth.

If a person of the same gender is not available, then, based on obligatory precaution, those of the opposite gender who are *mahram* to the deceased can perform it. *Mahram* means those relations with whom marriage is forbidden because of blood relationship or nursing (suckling) relationship or marriage, like brother and sister [or son-in-law and mother-in-law]. However, it is better that the washing be done with the body covered with a sheet of cloth.

Unity of gender is not required when giving ablution to a corpse of a child that had not reached the age of discerning the right and wrong.[46]

137. Based on obligatory precaution, the person performing ablution must be a *mu'min*.

---

[46] Translator's Note: The age of discerning right and wrong *(tamyíz)* is different from the age of maturity *(bulûgh)*. The latter is 9 for girls and 15 for boys but the former could be at five or six.

If neither a *mu'min* of the same gender as the deceased is available nor a *mahram* [even of the opposite gender], it is permissible that a Muslim of the same gender can wash the deceased.

If even a Muslim is not available, then the deceased can be washed by an Ahlul Kitãb person [that is, a Jew, a Christian or a Zoroastrian] of the same gender with the condition that that person should first wash himself and then perform ablution to the corpse.

If even an Ahlul Kitab person of the same gender is not available, the duty of performing ablution to the corpse is lifted, and the deceased should be buried without it.

[*Tahnít* and Shrouding]

138. After giving the ablution, it is wãjib to do *tahnít*. *Tahnít* means to rub camphour powder (which has maintained its fragrance) on the seven parts of the body that touch the ground in a posture of sajdah: the forehead, the palms, the knees, and feet toes. It is preferable to start *tahnít* with the forehead and end with the palms.

139. After *tahnít,* the deceased has to be shrouded in three pieces of cloth as follows:

(a) The *mi'zar:* a piece of cloth [like an apron] that must cover the body between the navel and the knees, based on obligatory precaution.

(b) The *qamís:* a piece of cloth [like a shirt] that must cover the body from the shoulders to mid shank, based on obligatory precaution.

(c) The *izãr:* a large sheet of cloth that must cover the entire body. Based on obligatory precaution, it must be long and wide enough so that the top and the bottom parts could be tied [with a string], and the front parts overlap.

[The Prayer]

140. It is obligatory to say prayer over a deceased Muslim's body of six years and over. Based on obligatory precaution, prayer should also be said over the body of a child who could do the *salāt* even if he or she had not yet reached the age of six.

141. The way to conduct prayer on the deceased:

The person praying should recite five *takbírs* (say "Allāhu Akbar").

However, it is preferable that after each *takbír* he says the following:

> After the first *takbir,* he should say the *shahādatayn* (declaration of faith in God and Prophet Muhammad).
>
> After the second *takbír,* he should say the *salawāt* on Prophet Muhammad (s.a.w.) and his progeny (a.s.).
>
> After the third *takbír,* he should say a prayer for the believing men and women.
>
> After the fourth *takbír,* he should say a prayer for the deceased.

He should say the fifth *takbír* and end the salāt.

[Burial]

142. It is necessary to bury the deceased after the salāt. Burial is intended to protect the body from wild animals and its smell is contained within so that no one is annoyed by it. The body should be placed on its right side with the face towards the *qiblah.*

143. It is not permissible to bury a deceased Muslim in the graveyard of non-Muslims, except if a section of that graveyard is specifically reserved for Muslims. Similarly, no non-Muslim can be buried in the graveyard of Muslims.

144. When it is neither possible to get a grave for a deceased Muslim in the graveyard of Muslims, nor transfer the body to a Muslim country for burial in a Muslim graveyard, that deceased Muslim may be buried in the graveyard of non-Muslims.

145. It has been narrated from the Prophet (s.a.w.) that he said, "No time comes upon the dead person more difficult than the first night [of burial]. Therefore have mercy on your dead ones by giving charity [on their behalf]. If one does not have anything [to give in charity], one of you should pray two *rak'ah* for them: in the first *rak'ah,* after al-Hamd, recite *Āyatu 'l-kursi;* and in the second rak'ah, after al-Hamd, recite surah al-Qadr ten times. After salām, say: *'Allāh humma salli 'alā Muhammadin wa Āli Muhammad, wab'ath thawābahā ila qabri fulān;'*[47] and name the deceased person [instead of *fulān*]."[48]

Question and Answers

146. Question: In some non-Muslim countries, the corpse is placed in a coffin and then buried in the grave. What is our duty in such a situation?

Answer: There is no problem in placing the corpse in a coffin when burying him in the ground. However, the religious requirements of burial must be fulfilled; and one of those requirements is that the corpse be placed on its right side with the face towards the *qiblah*.

147. Question: A Muslim died in a non-Muslim city that has no Muslim graveyard; and although it is possible to transfer the body to a Muslim country for burial but the cost of transportation is exorbitant—is this a sufficient [reason] for burying the body in the graveyard of non-Muslims?

---

[47] "O Allāh, send Your blessings upon Muhammad and the Family of Muhammad, and send the reward of this prayer to the grave of x."

[48] Sayyid as-Sistāni, *al-Masā'ilu 'l-Muntakhaba,* p. 63.

Answer: This is not a sufficient [reason].

148. Question: A Muslim dies in a non-Muslim city that has no Muslim graveyard and the family of the deceased cannot transfer the body to a Muslim country because it cannot afford the cost of transportation. In such cases, is it obligatory upon the Islamic centers that are responsible for Muslims' affairs to provide the cost of transportation? And is this obligatory upon the Muslims who reside in that city?

Answer: If burying the deceased in an appropriate grave in that same city or other city (excluding non-Muslim graveyards) depends on spending some money, and neither has he left any estate that can pay for it nor are the heirs capable of providing for it—then it is *wājib kifā'i* upon the Muslims to provide for it. And it is permissible to count it from the religious or charitable dues applicable to him.

149. Question: When there is no heir for a deceased Muslim person in a foreign land, who should take charge of his burial affairs?

Answer: If it is not possible to contact his heir and ask his consent in handling the burial procedures, the requirement of consent is lifted and it becomes obligatory, on basis of wajib *kifā'i,* on the Muslims to handle that affair.

150. Question: From where should the expenses of transportation to a Muslim country and burial come, if it is not possible to bury a Muslim in the city in which he died because there is no Muslim graveyard? Should these expenses come from the estate of the deceased before dividing it amongst the heirs? Or from the one-third [of the estate] if he has specified that? Or from other sources?

Answer: The expenses of burying a dead body in a place appropriate for it comes from the estate [before its distribution among the heirs] if he did not make a will specifying that it be taken from the one-third. Otherwise [if he made a will regarding the one-third], it should come out of it.

151. Question: The Muslim communities in non-Muslim countries are increasing day by day. Knowing the fact that a deceased Muslim will one day be buried in the graveyard of non-Muslims either because of lack of funds to available the family to send the dead body to Muslim countries for burial or because of negligence; so, is it obligatory, as a matter of *wājib kifā'i,* upon the capable Muslims to buy a graveyard for the Muslims?

Answer: Burying a deceased Muslim in a place appropriate to his status (other than non-Muslim graveyard) is an obligation of the heir just like other obligatory deeds connected with the burial procedures. And if the deceased has no heir or the heir is refusing to fulfill his duty or is not capable, it is obligatory, on basis of *kifā'i,* upon other Muslims [to bury the deceased in an appropriate place]. And if fulfilling this *wājib kifā'i* duty depends on acquiring a piece of land in advance by purchase or other means, it is obligatory to try and acquire in advance.

152. Question: What is preferable: burying a dead Muslim in an Islamic cemetery in a non-Muslim city in which he died or transferring the dead body to a Muslim city which entails exorbitant expenses?

Answer: It is preferable to transfer the dead to some of the holy shrines and other recommended places if there is a donar who can bear the expenses —from the heirs or others— or if the one-third of his estate which he has willed for religious charity, would suffice for that purpose. And Allāh knows the best.

153. Question: If transferring a deceased Muslim to Muslim countries entails great difficulty, is it permissible to bury him in cemeteries of non-Muslims from among the followers of the revealed religions [that is, Ahlul Kitāb]?

Answer: It is not permissible to bury a Muslim in cemeteries of non-Muslims, except if that is the only choice because necessity knows no laws.

* * *

PART TWO

* * * * * * * * * * *

FIQHUL MU'ĀMALĀT

PART TWO

1. Eating and Drinking.
2. Dress and Clothing.
3. Dealing with Laws in Non-Muslim Countries.
4. Work and Investment.
5. Interaction in Social Life.
6. The Medical Issues.
7. Marriage.
8. Women's Issues.
9. Youths' Issues.
10. Music, Singing and Dancing.
11. Miscellaneous.

Chapter One

EATING AND DRINKING

Introduction

Muslims [in predominantly Muslims countries] normally live in their own homes, villages and cities, in midst of their families and relations, eating variety of foods and drinking different drinks that they desire; They are familiar with the ingredients of these foods and know that it is free from all that their religion has forbidden, their faith has rejected, and their rich Islamic values have kept distance from. However, when they migrate to foreign countries to reside in the midst of non-Muslim communities, they are faced with problems in eating and drinking because they don't find foods that are familiar and desirable to them nor are their ingredients known to them. This is so because the host community is not Islamic, it has it own values, customs and habits which naturally do not abide by the laws of Islam. So when a Muslim desires to eat any food in a restaurant [in a non-Muslim country], he is faced with the problem of whether or not the food is permissible and pure.

General Rules

Here I wish to present some religious laws about food and drink that a Muslim should know, and then mention the specific questions and answers on that topic.

154. Since the followers of the **past revealed religions** (that is, the Jews, the Christians and the Zoroastrians) are ritually pure, many of the problems concerning the status and permissibility of the **food** are resolved when we live in their midst. It becomes permissible for us as Muslims to eat from their food no matter whether they touched it with their wet hands or not as long as we do not know or are not sure that it consists of what is forbidden to us, like intoxicating drinks.

As for meat, fat and their extracts, there are specific rules that will be discussed later on.

155. A Muslim is allowed to eat the food prepared by a **non-Muslim who is not from Ahlul Kitāb** [for example, a Hindu or a Buddhist] provided he does not know or is not sure that the non-Muslim touched the food with wetness; and provided he does not know or is not sure that the food consists of what is forbidden to him like intoxicating drinks.

As for meat, fat and their extracts, there are specific rules that will come later on.

156. A Muslim is allowed to eat any food made by a person about whose faith and religion is not known to him, no matter whether that person touched it with wetness or did not touch it, provided he does not know or is not sure that the food consists of what is forbidden to him.

As for meat, fat, and their extracts, there are specific rules that will come later on.

It is not necessary for the Muslim to question the **person who prepared the food** about his beliefs or disbeliefs, or whether he had touched the food or had not touch it, even if that inquiry is very convenient and natural for one who wants to ask.

In short, all kinds of food with the exception of meat, fat, and their extracts are permissible for a Muslim, even if he doubts that it might contain something which is forbidden for him to eat or doubts that its cook —whosoever he may be— had touched it with wetness. (See the question-answer section below.)

157. Just as it is not obligatory on him to inquire about the **ingredients** of such food to ensure that it is free from what is forbidden to him, it is not obligatory on him to ask the cook whether he touched it while preparing the food or after it.

158. All kinds of **packed food** with the exception of meat, fat and their extracts are permissible for a Muslim, even if he doubts that its ingredients might contain what is forbidden for him or even if he doubts that the cook —whosoever he may be— had touched it with wetness. It is not obligatory on him to inquire about its ingredients to ensure that it does not contain anything that is forbidden to him.

159. A Muslim is allowed to buy all kinds of *halāl* **meat** from a Muslim shopkeeper who sells it to Muslims.

Such meat would be considered *halāl* even if the vendor belongs to a school of thought which have different conditions for slaughtering from ours as long as there is a possibility that the animal was slaughtered in accordance with our conditions. This latter statement applies to all conditions except the one that says that the animal's belly should be facing the *qiblah* at the time of slaughter. Not observing the condition of *qiblah* because the slaughterer's school of thought does not consider it a necessity will not detract from [the permissibility of the meat].

160. If a Muslim knows and is sure that this meat is from an animal which is permissible for Muslim to eat (like cow, sheep or chicken) but that it is not slaughtered in accordance with Islamic laws, that meat is to be considered as *mayta*. *Mayta* is not permissible for a Muslim to eat even if its seller is a Muslim. Similarly, such meat is impure (*najis*) and would make other things impure if it comes into wet contact with it.

161. If a Muslim buys or receives meat from a non-Muslim, or from a Muslim who got it from a non-Muslim and did not inquire about its slaughtering according to Islamic laws, such meat is harãm for him.

But if the Muslim does not know that the animal was not slaughtered according to Islamic laws, it would not be considered *najis* although it is still *harãm*.

162. Some experts say that by letting out the blood by the method of slaughtering, the meat of the animal becomes healthier for the consumer than an animal that was not slaughtered. And so you should not be surprised to see some non-Muslims buying the meat that had been slaughtered according to Islamic laws from *halãl* meat stores.

163. In order for **fish** to become permissible for a Muslim, it must have the following two conditions:

    (a) The fish must have scales on it. [That is, it should not be a skin fish.]

    (b) The Muslim should be certain or satisfied that the fish has come out of the water alive or that it died while it was already in the fishing net.

It is not necessary for the fisherman to be a Muslim or to utter the name of Allãh for the fish to become *halãl*. So if a non-Muslim catches a fish and brings it alive from the water or it dies after getting caught in his fishing net or fishing line, and it has scales on it, it is permissible to eat that fish.

A Muslim can ascertain the first condition by examining the fish if it is being displayed or by observing its name [which can tell you whether it is a skin fish or a scale fish] as long as you can trust the authenticity of the label.

A list of scale fish has been appended at the end of this book.

The second condition is fulfilled in almost all the countries, as they say, because the universal method in fishing ensures that the fish comes out of the water alive or they die after coming into the fishing net.

Based on this, it is permissible to eat the fish that one gets from a non-Muslim just as one gets from a Muslim, no matter whether it is canned or uncanned. (See the question-answer section below.)

164. It is permissible to eat **shrimp** if it is brought out of the water alive.

It is forbidden to eat frogs, lobsters, turtles, every amphibious animal, snails, and crayfish. (See the question-answer section below.)

165. The law concerning **eggs of fish** follows the fish itself: the eggs of a *halāl* fish are permissible to eat and those of a *harām* fish are forbidden.

166. Some experts of fisheries say that scaleless fish mostly feed upon the waste of the sea and are in a way purifier of the filth, the squalor and the garbage of the sea.

167. It is forbidden to drink **wine, beer,** and everything that causes intoxication or drunkenness in solid or liquid form. Almighty Allāh says in the Qur'ān: *"O you who believe! Intoxicants and games of chance and (sacrificing to) stones set up and (dividing by) arrows are only an uncleanness, the Shatan's work; shut it therefore that you may be successful."* (5:90-91)

Our noble Prophet Muhammad (s.a.w.) said, "One who drinks intoxicants after Allāh has made them *harām* by my statement is not worthy of marriage [to your daughter] if he proposes to her, or of intercession when he asks for a good word, or of any credibility when he speaks, or of being entrusted with a trust."[49]

In another *hadíth*, he says, "Allāh has accursed alcohol, its growers, those who squeeze it [from the grapes], its drinkers, its servers, its buyers, its sellers, those who live on its income, its transporter, and the one to whom it is being transported."[50] There are many more *ahādíth* you will find in books of *hadíth* and jurisprudence.[51]

168. It is harām to **eat at the table** on which alcohol or any other intoxicants are being consumed. Based on obligatory precaution, it is harām to even **sit at** such a table. (See the question-answer section below.)

169. It is permissible for a Muslim to go to places where wine is being served with the food provided that does not lead to promotion of those restaurants.

However, he cannot eat from the table on which wine is being consumed and he should not, based on obligatory precaution, sit at that table.

There is no problem though, in sitting at a table near the table on which wine is being consumed.

170. It has been mentioned in the Chapter Three of Part One that all kinds of **alcohol** whether derived from wood or other sources are pure *(tāhir)*. Therefore, the food in whose preparation alcohol was used is *tāhir;* the liquids in which it

49 Al-Kulayni, Muhammad bin Ya'qûb, *Furû'u 'l-Kāfi*, vol. 6, p. 396.
50 As-Sadûq, *Man La Yahdhurhu 'l-Faqíh*, vol. 4, p. 4.
51 See *Furû'u 'l-Kāfi*, vol. 6, p. 396.

has been dissolved are also *tāhir*. (See the question-answer section below.)

171. It is harãm to use anything that **causes serious harm** to the human being like taking poison.

It is also harãm for a pregnant woman to drink something that would cause miscarriage.

Similarly, anything that is known to be harmful or supposed to be harmful or has the probability of harm [is also harãm] if that probability is considerable in the views of sensible people and that harm is serious enough to cause death or to disable a limb of the body.

172. There is **etiquette** to be observed at the dining table. Starting with the name of Allãh; eating with the right hand; making small morsels; sitting longer at the table; chewing the food well; thanking Allãh after the food; washing the fruits and vegetables before eating; not eating after satisfying the appetite; not over eating; not looking at the faces of others while eating; not taking away the food from others who are sitting at the table; and tasting the salt at the beginning and the end of the dinner.

Questions and Answers

173. **Question:** On the package of **meat** that is produced in Muslim countries by non-Muslim companies, it says, "slaughtered according to Islamic laws". Are we allowed to eat that meat? Can we eat that meat if it comes from Muslim companies in non-Muslim countries? And what is the ruling if the source is non-Muslim company from a non-Muslim country?

Answer: The writing [on the package] has no value at all.

If the producer is a Muslim or it was produced in a place where Muslims are in the majority and it is not known that the producer is a non-Muslim, then it is permissible to eat it.

But if the producer is a non-Muslim or it was produced in a place where Muslims are not in the majority and it is not known that the producer is Muslim, then it is not permissible to eat it.

174. Question: We enter some super markets in Europe and find meat in tin containers produced by a European company with the writing on the package that conveys the sense of it being "halāl" or "slaughtered according to Islamic laws". Is it permissible to buy and eat such meat?

Answer: The writing [on the package] has no value if it does not lead to surety [that it is actually halāl].

175. Question: Meat companies slaughter a large number of **chickens** at one time [that is, simultaneously]. Now if the person running the slaughtering machine is a Muslim, who says *takbír* and says the name of Allāh only once at the time of slaughtering all the chicken [simultaneously], is it permissible for us to eat those chickens? If we have doubt about these chickens being halāl, can we [ignore that doubt and] eat them and consider them pure *(tāhir)*?

Answer: If he repeats the name of Allāh as long as the machine is continuing to slaughter, it is sufficient. In the event of doubt about its being halāl (a doubt which arises concerning the mentioning of the name of Allāh), it can be considered pure and can be consumed.

176. Question: Is it permissible to buy meat thinking that it is slaughtered according to Islamic laws from a super-market owned by a Muslim who [also] sells alcoholic drinks?

Answer: Yes, it is permissible; and it is halāl to eat it even if it previously came from a non-Muslim as long as there is a likelihood that the shopkeeper has ascertained that it was slaughtered according to the *shari'a* laws; but not if there is no such likelihood.

177. Question: Some of the **cheese** manufactured in non-Muslim countries contain **rennet** extracted from the calf or other animals. We do not know whether the rennet was taken from the animal that was slaughtered according to Islamic laws; neither do we know that it has transformed into something else. So is it permissible to eat such cheese?

Answer: There is no problem in eating such cheese.

178. Question: Gelatin is used in a number of drinks and food items in the west. We do not know that gelatin has been extracted from a vegetable or an animal source; and that if it is from an animal, is it from its bones or from the tissues around the bones; neither do we know if the animal was one that is halāl for us or harām. Are we allowed to eat such a gelatin?

Answer: It is permissible to eat if the doubt is whether it has been extracted from an animal or a vegetable.

But if it is known that it was derived from an animal, then it is not permissible to eat without ascertaining that the animal was slaughtered according to *sharī'a*. This prohibition applies, as a matter of obligatory precaution, even if it was extracted from animal bones.

Of course, if a chemical change occurs in the original ingredients during the process of manufacturing the gelatin, there is no problem at all in eating it. Similarly, even if one has doubt whether the animal was slaughtered Islamically or not, still there is no problem in adding the gelatin [made from that animal] to the food in such a minute amont that it is completely absorbed in it.

179. Question: Commercial fishing vessels place their huge nets [in the sea] and catch tons of **fish** which are then sold in the markets. It is well known that modern methods of fishing are based on catching the fish alive, and that the fishermen throw the dead fish back into the water for fear of contamination.

Therefore, is it permissible for us to buy such fish in the markets of non-Muslims? Is it permissible for us to buy such fish from Muslims who are not considerate of religious laws? In both the cases to ascertain that this particular, fish in front of me was taken out of the water alive, should seek the advice of an expert and reliable witness to testify to that fact which may prove difficult, impractical, and unrealistic.

So is there a solution for practicing Muslims who face difficulty in ascertaining whether or not the meat of chicken, cow or sheep is halāl, and therefore take to eating fish instead?

Answer: There is no problem in buying it from Muslim or non-Muslims; as there is no problem in eating it if they are satisfied that the fish was caught by the method mentioned above and that it belongs to the category of scale fish.

180. Question: At times we find the name or picture of fish on the cans and come to know that the fish is a scale fish. So is it permissible for us to rely on the name or the picture in determining the category of fish knowing well that a wrong statement of this kind would put the manufacturers in great loss or even more serious [situation] than just a loss?

Answer: If one is satisfied its truth, it is permissible to act upon it.

181. Question: Is it permissible to eat **lobster**, in all its varieties, by following the pattern of shrimp?

Answer: It is not permissible to eat lobster.

182. Question: Is it permissible to buy a fish from a Muslim who is not a Shi'a while we have no knowledge whether it is from the category of scale fish or not?

Answer: It is permissible to buy it but one cannot eat it unless he ascertains that it is from the category of scale fish.

183. Question: Is it permissible to eat halāl food which has been steam cooked with the steam of meat not slaughtered according to Islam?

Answer: It is not permissible since the food, as mentioned in the question, will be considered impure *(najis)* because of coming into contact with the wet parts from the steam of the impure meat.

184. Question: If **wine is served at a table**, it is harām for a Muslim to seat at that table. What is meant by "table"? Does this apply to the entire group [that has gone to the restaurant and some are being served alcohol] even if the tables are more than one? Or does it only apply to one table [and not the group] in the sense that if there are two separate tables, it is would be permissible to sit [at the table on which alcohol is not being served, even if they are part of the same company]?

Answer: The criterion is one table. However, one should know that the prohibition of sitting at a table on which wine or intoxicant drinks are being served is based on precaution; of course, eating and drinking at that table is harām based on obligatory precaution.

185. Question: A Muslim enters a café and sits down at a table to drink tea, then a stranger comes at the same table to drink wine. Is it obligatory upon the Muslim to stop drinking tea and leave?

Answer: Yes, as mentioned earlier, it is obligatory to move away from that table.

186. Question: Is it permissible to drink the **beer** that says "alcohol free" on it?

Answer: It is not permissible to drink if "beer" means the drink made from barley that causes mild drunkenness. But if it means a drink made from barley that does not cause mild drunkenness, there is no problem in it.

187. Question: Alcohol is used in the production of many drugs and medications: Is it permissible to take them? Are they considered pure *(tāhir)*?

Answer: They are pure; and since the alcohol used in them is so minute that it dissolves in them, it is therefore permissible to take them also.

188. Question: There is this **vinegar** that is made from wine in the sense that it was wine and then, through a manufacturing process, changed into vinegar. Therefore, the label on the bottle reads: "wine vinegar" as opposed to the vinegar made from barley or other items. One of the signs [of differentiating between "wine vinegar" and the wine itself is that] the bottles of this vinegar are displayed in the area of vinegar, and it has never happened that these bottles be placed on the shelves of wines. Moreover, there is no difference between such vinegar and the vinegar made from dates for example.

So can this wine which has turned into vinegar be considered vinegar under the rule of change *(inqilāb)*?

Answer: If the name "vinegar" can be applied in the view of common people upon that product, as has been assumed in the question, the same rule governing vinegar would apply to it. [That is, it is pure as well as permissible.]

189. Question: The manufacturers of food and sweets as well as of the food packed in cans are required to mention the ingredients of the items being sold. To prevent the food from going bad, manufacturers add **preservatives** to them; these preservatives could be from animal source and are listed by alphabetical codes like "E" alongside a number like "E 450" or "E 472," etc.

What is the ruling in the following situations?

(a) When one does not know the origin of these preservatives?

(b) If one sees a list issued by those who have no idea of the rule of chemical transformation (*istihālah:* a purifying agent) that says that the items described by so and so alphabet and/or number are forbidden because they come from animal source?

(c) When one does preliminary research and is satisfied that the preservative agent does not retain its original form but transforms in characteristics and changes into another substance?

Answer:

(a) It is permissible to eat the food containing those preservatives.

(b) If it is not ascertained that it is from an animal source —even if such a claim is made— it is permissible to eat it. Similarly, [it is permissible] if it is ascertained that [it is from an animal source] but one is uncertain whether it comes from an impure *mayta* and that its amount mixed in the food stuff is so minute that it is completely absorbed in it in the view of common people.

(c) There is no problem in applying the rule of purity and permissibility whenever the chemical change is proved in the form that it transforms into another substance and in the view of common people nothing of the original substance remains.

190. Question: It is requested of you to answer the following two questions:

(a) Is **gelatin** by itself considered pure *(tāhir)*?

(b) If we have doubt whether or not *istihāla* (chemical change) has occurred [in the process of manufacturing the gelatin] because of uncertainty about the concept and the extent of applying the rule of *istihāla,* do we extend the previous knowledge *(istishāb)* that gelatin is still impure?

Answer:

(a) As for the gelatin derived from animal source, if the impurity of the origin is not established (for example, if there is a probability that the animal was slaughtered according to Islam), it will be considered pure; however, it should not be added to the food, except in such amounts that it would be completely absorbed. [That is, it is pure *(tāhir)* but should be used in food items in very minute quantities only.]

This [latter caution] is for a case where it is neither established that the animal was slaughtered according to Islam nor had *istihāla* taken place. [If any of these two issues were established, then there would be no restriction in using gelatin in food items.]

The above ruling does not differ whether the gelatin was derived from parts of the animal that has feeling (like cartilage, gristle) or has no feeling (like bones). This ruling about parts with no feeling is based on obligatory precaution.

However, if its impurity was established (for example, it is known that it comes from an essentially impure animal or from cartilage of an animal not slaughtered according to Islam or from its bones without purifying them, in which case it would be considered *mutanajjis* by coming into wet contact with an impure item), then considering it as pure and permissible for use in food items depends on establishing *istihāla*. And in this matter [whether *istihāla* took place or not], one should refer to the common perception of the people. We have explained its criterion earlier.

(b) [*Istishāb* is a principle that says that in case of doubt one should extend the previous knowledge about that particular issue until proven otherwise.] The principle of *istishāb* is neither applicable in cases of doubt concerning the concept [of the law] nor in cases of the law themselves—as has been proven in its appropriate place in the Science of

'Usûl. However, since the issue of impurity *(najāsat)* is related to the generic concept in a common man's perspective and extension of judgement about *najāsat* depends, in the eyes of reasonable people, on continued existence of its elements — this makes the doubt about occurrence of *istihāla* (whether its application is limited or broad) into a doubt about continued existence of impure elements [in the gelatin]. And this is a matter of application of the law, therefore, there is no problem in applying the principle of *istishāb* in this case. Allāh knows the best.

191. Question: We are unaware of the ingredients of food sold in shops in Western countries: it might be free from those ingredients that are forbidden to us or it might contain them. Are we allowed to eat such items **without looking into their ingredients,** or inquiring about them? Or is that not allowed to us?

Answer: It is permissible [to eat such food] as long as it is not known that it contains meat, fat, and their derivatives that are forbidden to us.

192. Question: Is it permissible to use, in our foods, the **oils** derived from fish that are forbidden to us? What about using such oils in other than food?

Answer: It is not permissible to eat such oils but their other usage is permissible. Allāh knows the best.

193. Question: Is it permissible for a Muslim **to attend** a gathering where **intoxicant drinks** are being served?

Answer: Eating and drinking in those gatherings is forbidden. However, the prohibition in attending such gatherings is based on compulsory precaution. But there is no problem in attending such gatherings for purpose of forbidding the evil *(nahi 'anil munkar)*, if one is capable of doing that.

194. Question: It is permissible to eat lobster, crayfish, and snails?

Answer: Is it not permissible to eat from marine animals anything except fish that has scale; shrimp is considered from that category [of permissible sea animals]. But other than fish, like lobster, and similarly the fish that does not have scale is forbidden. Allāh knows the best.

* * *

Chapter Two

DRESS AND CLOTHING

Introduction

Wearing clothes made of natural leather is a real problem for Muslims living in non-Muslim countries. Muslims are used to buying leather products in their own countries without any problem at all because they know that they are made from leather that comes from animals that have been slaughtered according to Islamic laws. So they wear them, pray in them, and touch them with their wet hands without any problem or hesitation.

But in non-Muslim countries, the reality is completely different.

General Rules

195. **Leather products** are impure *(najis)* and salãt in them is not permissible, if we know that they have been made from the hide of an animal not slaughtered according to Islamic laws.

Such products are considered pure and salat in them is permissible if there is a probability that they were made from skin of an animal that is essentially *halãl* and was slaughtered according to Islamic laws

Salãt is not permissible in leather products made from **skin of predatory animals** like lion, leopard, tiger, fox, and jackal. Similarly, based on obligatory precaution, salat is not permissible in leather products made from non-predatory animals whose meat is forbidden to us like monkeys and elephants even though their hide could be considered *tãhir* if they certainly were (or there is a probability that they were) killed according to Islamic laws.

In all these cases of probability, wearing a **belt** and things like that made from leather is allowed [in salãt] provided that they are not big enough to conceal the private parts.

If there exists no probability that it was slaughtered according to Islamic laws, and, on the contrary, we are sure that it comes from skin of an animal that was not slaughtered according to Islamic law, then it is *najis* and salãt in it is not permissible. [With no such probability,] even the use of belt and other things (that cannot conceal the sexual organs in salãt) is not permissible on the basis of obligatory precaution. It would be the same law if the probability waw very low that sensible people ignore it (for example, 2%).

The permissibility of the leather of these animals can be achieved by two methods: The first method is that they be slaughtered just as a sheep is slaughtered with all conditions observed. The second method is that they are hunted by using a gun. In the latter case, the hunter must be a Muslim; he must invoke Allāh's name while pulling the trigger; he must shoot with the purpose of hunting, and get to the place where the animal fell after it has died or when there was not enough time to slaughter it.

197. Leather products made in non-Muslim countries from **hides of snakes and crocodiles** and displayed in non-Muslims markets are considered pure *(tāhir)*; and it is permissible to buy, sell, and use them in things that require purity.

198. Leather products made in Muslim countries and displayed in non-Muslim markets are considered pure *(tāhir)* and it is permissible to use them in *salāt.*

199. Leather products made in non-Muslim countries about which we are uncertain whether they are from natural or synthetic leather are considered pure and it is permissible to use them in *salāt.*

200. Shoes made from leather of an animal not slaughtered according to Islamic laws do not make the feet *najis* except through wetness that transfers the impurity. So if the foot sweats and the sock becomes soaked with the sweat, yet the latter does not reach the impure leather, it will not make the foot or the sock impure.

201. It is permissible to say salāt with a leather cap or a leather belt manufactured in non-Muslim countries and bought in non-Muslim markets if there is a probability that these leather products were made from hide of animals that are essentially halāl and were slaughtered according to Islamic laws. This has been mentioned in the third rule of this section. (See the question-answer section below.)

202. Men are not allowed to wear **gold** regardless whether it is a [normal] ring or a wedding ring or a wristwatch or other things in salāt as well as outside it.

It is permissible for them to wear gold-plated items provided that gold is only considered as a coating and nothing more.

203. It is permissible for men to wear what is known as white gold.

204. Women are allowed to wear gold at all times, even in salāt.

205. Men are not allowed to wear pure and natural **silk**, neither in salāt nor outside salāt, except under special circumstances that have been explained in the books of Islamic jurisprudence.

206. Women are allowed to wear silk at all times even in salāt.

207. Men are allowed to wear 'doubtful' silk fabrics and clothes about whose origin there is no certainty, i.e. whether they are made from natural silk or synthetic one. In this case, even salāt in it is permissible. (See the question-answer section below.)

Similarly, it is permissible for them to wear natural silk that has been blended with other material like cotton, wool, nylon, etc. to an extent that the blended fabric is no longer considered pure silk. This law also applies if there is uncertainty about the extent of blending [of pure silk and other material]. In such cases, it is also permissible to say salāt in it.

208. Based on obligatory precaution, men are not allowed to dress up in women's clothes.

209. Based on obligatory precaution, muslims are not allowed to dress up in clothes that are specifically known as the dress of non-Muslims.

Questions and Answers

210. **Question:** We Muslims in Europe buy shoes, belts and other clothing items made from leather which may come from animals killed in non-Islamic way. At times such items are imported from Muslim countries or obtained from Muslim abattoirs here (since there are a few Muslim abattoirs in the U.K. for example).

Can we consider such leather to be pure *(tāhir)* in the probability that it might have been imported from Muslim countries or obtained from abattoirs adopting Islamic way of slaughtering, even if such a probability is very weak?

Answer: If the probability is so weak that the opposite is more likely (for example, 2%), it should not even be considered. Otherwise [if the probability is high], there is no problem in considering it to be pure *(tāhir)*. Allāh knows the best.

211. Question: Jurists have decreed that it is forbidden [for men] to wear pure and natural silk.

Is it permissible for a man to wear silk that is mixed with other material if that clothing item is a **necktie** [or the normal tie]? And is it forbidden for man to wear the necktie if it is made from natural and pure silk?

Answer: It is not forbidden to wear a **tie** even if it is from pure silk because it is not [big enough material] to cover the private parts that must be covered [in prayer].

As for the item that is mixed with other material to an extent that it cannot be described as "pure silk," it is permissible to wear it even if it [is big enough so that it] can cover the private parts that must be covered [in prayer].

212. Question: Even though some manufacturers write on their products that they have been made from natural silk, we doubt such a claim because of the goods very low price. Is it permissible for us to wear such an item and say salāt in it?

Answer: With doubt [whether the silk is pure], it is permissible to wear it and say salāt in it.

213. Question: Is it permissible to wear clothes that have pictures of intoxicating drinks as a promotion for drinking them? Is it permissible to sell such items?

Answer: It is forbidden to wear and sell them.

214. Question: Is it permissible for a man to wear a watch that contains parts made from gold or a watch whose strap is made of gold? Is it permissible to say salāt with it?

Answer: It is permissible to wear the first item and pray in it but not the second.

* * *

Chapter Three

DEALING WITH LAWS IN NON-MUSLIM COUNTRIES

Introduction

Various governments lay down laws to govern the conduct of the lives of their citizens, at times they would order people to do something and at times prohibit them from doing some other things; they would limit and restrict certain activities, etc.

Among those laws are the laws concerning public utilities related to daily lives of the people in a given geographical area; and violating or disobeying these laws could led to disarray and chaos.

General Rules

Therefore, it is appropriate to clarify the following issues.

215. It is not permissible for anyone to leave something on the **public road** that could cause harm to the pedestrians and others anywhere in Muslim and non-Muslim countries.

216. It is not permissible for a Muslim to **post bills** or write or engage in other similar activities on the outer walls or billboards that are owned by others except after obtaining the permission of the owner.

217. It is forbidden for a Muslim to **betray the trust** of someone who has entrusted him with an item or a deed even if that person happens to be a non-Muslim.

It is similarly obligatory upon a Muslim to safeguard the deposit that has been given to him and give it back in full. Therefore, one who works as a cashier or accountant is not allowed to betray the employer and steal something that is under his control.[52] (See the question-answer section below.)

218. It is neither permissible to **steal** from the private as well as the public property of non-Muslims nor to **vandalize** it even if that stealing or vandalizing does not tarnish the image of Islam and Muslims. Such an act is counted as perfidy and violation of the guarantee given to non-Muslims indirectly when one asked permission to enter or reside in that country. And it is forbidden to breach the trust and violate the guarantee in regard to every person irrespective of his religion, citizenship, and beliefs. (See the question-answer section below.)

219. It is not permissible to steal the property of non-Muslims when they enter Muslim countries.

---

[52] *Dalīlu 'l-Muslim fi Bilādi 'l-Ghurba*, p. 89-90.

220. It is not permissible for a Muslim to receive wages and subsidy through illegal means, and other similar methods, for example, by **giving false information** to the authorities.

221. It is permissible for a Muslim to purchase **insurance policy** from various insurance companies for insuring his life and property from fire, flood, theft, and other perils. The insurance agreement is considered as a binding contract and cannot be cancelled except by consent of both parties.

222. It is not permissible for a Muslim to give false information to the insurance companies with the purpose of obtaining something that he is not entitled to just as he is not allowed to intentionally stage an accident like fire, for example, in order to gain something nor would the insurance benefits be lawful for him. (See the question-answer section below.)

223. At times the higher interests of the Muslims in non-Muslim countries demand that Muslims seek membership of **political parties**, enter parliaments, and representative assemblies. In such cases, it is permissible for Muslims to engage in such activities as much as is demanded by the interest [of the Muslim community] that must be identified by consulting the trustworthy experts.

224. Under no circumstance is it permissible to **cheat in school exams** irrespective of the fact that cheating is done by mutual help among the students or by the passing of notes or by duping the inspector and other illegal methods that are against the [education] system. (See the question-answer section below).

Questions and Answers

225. Question: If a Muslim tries to get from bank's cash dispensing machine some of his own money and more money than what he had asked for is dispensed, is he allowed to take the extra money without the bank knowing about it?

Answer: It is not allowed.

226. Question: A Muslim buys a commodity from a foreign company in a non-Muslim country; the seller by mistake gives more than what was ordered. Is the Muslim customer allowed to take the extra? Is he obliged to inform the seller about the mistake?

Answer: It is not lawful for him to take the extra; if he did so, it is obligatory for him to return it.

227. Question: A Muslim employee of a non-Muslim company is in a position to misappropriate company's products. Is he allowed to do this?

Answer: It is not permissible.

228. Question: Is it permissible to tamper with electric or water or gas meters, in non-Muslim countries?

Answer: This also is not permissible.

229. Question: A Muslim in the West claims that he used to drive in his country for many years and supports his claim with a document from a given source so that he gets a preferable rate for his insurance premium. Is he allowed to change the fact in his statement even if it is by *tawriya* method? Is it permissible to help him for this purpose?

Answer: Lying for the above mentioned purpose is not permissible nor is it allowed to claim money in this way; and helping in this is helping in committing a sin.

230. Question: Is it permissible to cheat insurance companies in non-Muslim countries when one is confident that it would not tarnish the image of Islam and Muslims?

Answer: It is not permissible.

231. Question: A Muslim deliberately tourches his insured house so that he may receive compensation from the non-Muslim insurance company. Is he allowed to do this? And is it permissible for him to receive the compensation?

Answer: It is not permissible for him to destroy and waste the property, nor is it allowed for him to give false information to the insurance company for the purpose mentioned above. The money received [in this process] is not lawful.

232. Question: Is it permissible to cheat [in the exams] at public schools in Europe? Is it permissible to cheat [in the exams] at the private Islamic and non-Islamic schools?

Answer: Cheating is not allowed in any of these [schools].

233. Question: In some means of transportation, there are signs that say, "No Smoking". Is it permissible to disobey those signs?

Answer: If that sign is like an additional condition for riding in that vehicle or it is an official by-law of the government, and the passenger has given commitment to abide by the official laws, it is necessary for him to act according to that condition and his commitment.

234. Question: Is it necessary for the person who has got a visa to enter a non-Muslim country to abide by the laws of that country in all fields, like traffic laws, laws regarding work and employment, etc.?

Answer: If he has given them a commitment —even if indirectly [as is implied in the immigration documents]— to abide by the laws of that country, it is necessary for him to fulfill his commitment in issues that are not contrary to the sacred laws [of Islam].

As for example, for traffic regulations, it is necessary to obey them regardless [of the fact whether you have given a commitment or not] if not obeying those rules could eventually lead to harming people's lives and properties which are sacrosanct [in Islamic laws].

235. Question: Some governments offer social security benefits to their citizens as long as one does not find a job. Is it permissible for them to continue receiving these benefits, even after they have found work and have not informed the department concerned about it?

Answer: It is not permissible for them to accept the benefits except after informing the competent authorities in those countries about it.

236. Question: Is it permissible for a Muslim to steal from non-Muslims in non-Muslim countries?

And is it permissible for him to cheat them in methods that are common among themselves in order to acquire their property?

Answer: It is not permissible to steal, their private or public property, or to vandalize it if that leads to tarnishing the image of Islam or Muslims in general.

Similarly, it is not allowed to steal even if it does not lead to that [i.e., tarnishing the image of Islam or Muslims] but is considered as perfidy and violation of the guarantee given to non-Muslims indirectly when one asked permission to enter or reside in their country. And it is forbidden to breach the trust and violate the guarantee in regard to every person.

237. **Question:** Is it permissible for a Muslim to give false information to government agencies in Europe in order to gain monetary and non-monetary privileges and benefits through their lawful means?

Answer: It is not permissible because it is lying; and what has been mentioned is not a justified reason [for lying].

* * *

Chapter Four

WORK AND INVESTMENT

Introduction

As a principal, it is permissible for a Muslim to engage as an employee of a non-Muslim in various vital activities of life and in different kinds of work of general benefit so that he may be useful to himself and to humanity. This permission is conditional to the fact that such work has not been forbidden by the laws of Islam and that it does not lead to harming the interest of Muslims or to serve the interest and schemes of the enemies of Islam and Muslims.

General Rules

239. It is not permissible for a Muslim to debase himself in front of any human being be they Muslim or non-Muslim. So if the work that a Muslim does debases him in from of a non-Muslim, it is not permissible for him to engage in that debasing work.

240. A Muslim is allowed to **serve meat** of an animal that was not slaughtered according to Islamic laws to those who consider it lawful like Christians, Jews, and others.

Similarly, it is permissible for him to work in preparing and cooking of that meat. The money that he receives in return for that work can be legitimized by the rule of *tanāzul* (withdrawing your exclusive right from that meat).

241. It is not permissible for a Muslim to **sell pork** to those who believe it is lawful for them from among the Christians and others. Based on obligatory precaution, one should not even serve that meat to them. (See the question-answer section below.)

242. A Muslim is not allowed to **serve intoxicating drinks** to anyone at all, even to those who believe it is lawful to them. He is not [even] allowed to wash the dishes or give them to others if that washing and giving is part of the drinking of intoxicants.

243. A Muslim is not allowed to hire himself out for selling or serving intoxicating drinks or for washing the dishes for that purpose just as it is not allowed for him to take the wages for this work, as it is unlawful.

As for the "extreme need" justification used by some people for these kind of work, it is an unacceptable justification. Almighty Allāh says, *"And whosoever is careful of (his duty towards) Allāh, He will make for him an outlet;*

and give him in sustenance from whence he thinks not. And
whosoever trusts in Allāh, He is sufficient for him..." (65:3)
He also said, *"Surely those whom the angels cause to die while
they are unjust to their themselves, they shall say, 'In what
state were you?' They shall answer, 'We were weak in the
earth.' They shall say, 'Was not Allāh's earth spacious so that
you should have migrated therein?' So these it is whose abode
is hell, and it is an evil resort except the weak from among the
men and the children who have not in their power the means
nor can they find a way (to escape)."* (4:97-98)

In his sermon of the last pilgrimage, Prophet Muhammad
(s.a.w.) said, "Know that the Trustworthy Soul (Jibra'il) has
inspired in my mind that no soul shall die until its sustenance
is completed. Therefore fear Allāh and work hard in seeking
[the sustenance]; and let not the delay in getting your share of
the sustenance compel you to seek it through disobeying Allāh
for the Blessed and Almighty Allāh has divided the sustenance
among His creation by lawful means and not through unlawful
means. So whosoever fears Allāh and has patience, Allāh will
provide them sustenance from lawful [means]; but whosoever
tears apart the curtain of propriety, makes haste and acquire
their portion from unlawful [means], it will be taken off from
their lawful sustenance and they will be held accountable for it
on the day of resurrection."[53] (See the question-answer section
below.)

244. It is not permissible to work in places of
entertainment and other similar places of debauchery if that
work would cause one to drift towards unlawful acts. (See the
question-answer section below.)

245. It is permissible for Muslims to participate as
partners with non-Muslims (like Christians and Jews for
example) in various kinds of businesses considered lawful in

---

[53]   Al-Hurr al-'Āmili, *Wasā'ulu 'sh-Shí'a,* vol. 17, p. 44.

Islamic laws like selling, buying, export, import, building contracts, etc.

246. It is permissible **to deposit** [money] in non-Muslim (private or state-owned) banks.

247. If a Muslim intends **to get a loan** from such banks, it is necessary that he should do so with the intention that it is a transaction without return, even if he knows that he will end up paying the capital as well as the interest. And he should not do so with the intention of getting the loan with the condition of interest.

248. It is permissible for a Muslim to authorise another person to use his name (and his credit) to buy shares, in return for an amount (in money or commodity) on which both have reached an agreement.

249. It is not permissible for a Muslim to buy products of the countries that are in a state of war with Islam and Muslims, for example, Israel. (See the question-answer section below.)

250. A Muslim is allowed to **exchange the currency** with some other currency at the market price, or at a lower or higher rate, irrespective of the fact that the exchange is of an immediate or a deferred nature.

251. It is forbidden to use bank-notes that are **counterfeit** or have no value at all—the money that is used by a fraudester when he pays the worker who is unaware of its forgery or worthlessness. The business deal conducted with this kind of money is not valid.

252. [a] It is not permissible for a Muslim to buy tickets of chance (including **lottery**) if he buys them with the intention of luckily winning the prize.

[b] It is permissible for him to buy the lottery tickets if he buys it with the intention of participating in a charitable cause that is accepted Islamically like building hospitals, orphanages, etc., but not with the intention of winning the

prize. However, this hypothetical situation is extremely difficulty to occur in non-Muslim countries that consider certain activities that are forbidden in Islam to be of a charitable cause according to their own understanding.

In both the cases [of "a" and "b" if a Muslim wins the lottery], it is permissible to receive the prize from a non-Muslim [person or company]. (See the question-answer section below.)

253. It is permissible to sell wild animals whose meat is forbidden like tiger, hyena, fox, elephant, lion, bear, and other similar animals like cat and whale fish if there is any permissible benefit which makes them valuable in the market (even if in view of only some experts of that field). Non-hunting dogs and pigs are exempt from this rule. (See the question-answer section below.)

254. It is permissible to sell and buy **gold and silver utensils** for the purpose of decoration; however, it is forbidden to use them for eating and drinking.

255. No *khums* is levied on the salary paid by a government in a Muslim country directly into the bank account of its employee, even if it is more than his annual expenses—as long as he does not receive it in his hands. (See the question-answer no. 260 section below.)

Questions and Answer

256. Question: In the West, it is possible for a person to open a variety of current accounts with high or low **interest rates** equally without any difficulty in both the cases.

Is it permissible to open accounts with high interest rate with the understanding that the person will not demand the interest, if the bank denies it to him?

If it is not permissible, is there a solution that would allow them to open such an account knowing well that they, in their heart, are seeking the best interest?

Answer: They are allowed to open the account in the bank and it is [also] permissible for them to deposit in it with the condition of earning the interest if the bank is financed by non-Muslim governments or people.

257. Question: Banks in the West give loans —known as **mortgage**— to those who do not have enough money to buy houses; this is to be paid back in [weekly or monthly] instalments with a high rate of interest.

Is a Muslim allowed to use this facility? If it is not permissible, is there a solution in your view for someone who claims that he needs the mortgage to buy his own residential house and does not possess enough money to pay for it?

Answer: It is permissible to take the money from the bank that is financed by non-Muslim government or private funds but not with the intention of loan. The knowledge that the bank will sooner or later force him to pay the capital as well as the interest does not affect [the lawfulness of] his taking the money.

258. Question: Some governments are committed to providing housing for the needy under specific circumstances. Is it permissible for a Muslim to buy a house in which he resides for a short time (so that he will not be liable for *khums* [on that house]), and then he gives it out on rent so he can then go and live in a house subsidized by the government?

Answer: *Khums* is not waived from a house just by living in it for a short while without actually being in need of it, as has been presumed in the question.

259. Question: Some trading and manufacturing companies get loans from private or state banks in Muslim countries and also from other [non-Muslim] institutions with the condition of interest; and they also earn interest on the deposits they leave in those banks. Are we allowed to buy shares from these companies or be partners in their ventures?

Answer: If the partnership with them is like participating in their interest-bearing activities, it is not allowed. However, if Muslims own the company and it receives interest from the banks of non-Muslims, there is no problem [in buying its shares or partnership] from this perspective.

260. Question: Some governments and some companies in non-Muslim as well as Muslim countries deposit the salaries of their employees directly into their accounts in the banks. The employee does not get the money in his hand, although he can withdraw it whenever he wants. Now if the statement of his account shows that the money has surpassed his annual expenses, is *khums* obligatory on it?

Answer: *Khums* is obligatory in what has surpassed his annual needs, except in the case of a government employee in a Muslim state that deposits his salary into a state or private bank. In the latter case, *khums* would not be obligatory on the salary that has been deposited in the bank until he [physically] takes possession of it with the permission of the mujtahid.[54] Then the salary will be included in his income of that year and *khums* will become obligatory on what is in excess to that year's expenses.

261. Question: If a Muslim takes a loan from another Muslim and then after some time the market value of that amount goes down, so how much should he pay back to the creditor? The amount that he got as loan or its equivalent in

---

[54] Translator's Note: Working for a government in a Muslim state is itself problematic from the religious point of view unless it is an Islamic government. So the salary received from such a government cannot become legitimate unless permission is sought from the mujtahid. This is the underlining reason for the clause "without the permission of the mujtahid" in the above answer.

the market value at the time of payment? Does the rule differ if the creditor was a non-Muslim?

Answer: He has to pay the same amount that he got as loan; and there is no difference whether the creditor was a Muslim or a non-Muslim.

262. Question: Is it permissible to invest in companies some of whose products are intoxicanting drinks without the possibility of separating one's investment from that of the others in that line of production?

Answer: It is not permissible to participate or deal in production of intoxicanting drinks.

263. Question: A Muslim builder or contractor is approached for building a place of worship for non-Muslims in a non-Muslim country. Is it permissible for him to accept that job?

Answer: It is not permissible because it involves promoting the false religions.

264. Question: A Muslim calligrapher is approached for preparing a billboard promoting intoxicanting drinks or for an all-night dance party or for a restaurant that serves pork. Is it permissible for him to accept these jobs?

Answer: It is not permissible because it involves advertising indecent acts and promoting immorality.

265. Question: Is it permissible to buy from shops that dedicate part of their profits to supporting Israel?

Answer: We do not allow that.

266. Question: A Muslim buys a building but does not know that it also contains a pub whose lease he cannot terminate [before its expiry]. Then he finds out the fact.

(One) Is it permissible for him to receive the rent of the pub from the lessee?

(Two) If it is not allowed, is it permissible for him to receive the rent with the permission of the mujtahid? Or under other pretext?

(Three) If we assume that he knew about the existence of the pub before buying the building, is it permissible for him to buy that building knowing that he cannot terminate the lease of the pub owner?

Answer:

(a) It is not permissible for him to receive the rent in return for renting that place as a pub.

(b) Since he owns the right of rent of that place for permissible use, it is allowed for him to take (from the money given to him as rent for the pub) an amount that is his right. If the lessee is a non-Muslim, the owner can take the money but not as rent [for the pub].

(c) It is permissible for him to buy that building even if he knew about the above-mentioned lessee and that he cannot terminate that lease.

267. Question: Is it permissible for a Muslim business owner to employ non-Muslims in his business even though there are Muslims who need jobs?

Answer: On its own terms, it is permissible; but based on the demands of Islamic brotherhood and the rights that Muslims have over one another, it is better to choose Muslims over non-Muslims as long as there is no problem in it.

268. Question: Is it permissible to work as salesman or cashier in shops that sell pornographic magazines? Is it permissible to deal in these kinds of magazines? Is it permissible to print them?

Answer: None of these [activities] is permissible because it means promoting forbidden acts and propagating immorality.

269. Question: A Muslim works in a non-Muslim country in a private office or in a government office or on contract for a specific project where he is paid by the hour. Is it permissible for him to waste some hours or work negligently or intentionally delay the job? Does he deserve the full wages?

Answer: This is not allowed; and if one does that, he is not entitled to full wages.

270. Question: Some Muslims deal in the **manuscripts** of the Holy Qur'ān which they import from Muslim countries. Is this permissible? If the obstacle in selling is the law that forbids selling the Qur'ān to non-Muslims, is it possible to bypass this condition so that the deal may be legitimate? If it is permissible, how do we bypass this condition?

Answer: We do not allow this since it is detrimental to the [intellectual and cultural] heritage of the Muslims and their resources.

271. Question: Is it permissible to deal in manuscripts, art works, and Islamic artifacts by importing them from Muslim countries with the purpose of selling them at high prices in, for example, European countries? Or is this considered ruinous to Islamic heritage, and therefore not permissible?

Answer: We do not allow this for the reason mentioned earlier.

272. Question: During some nights the clubs are filled with their non-Muslim customers who usually get drunk, and come out looking for restaurants to eat their meal. Is it permissible for a Muslim to work in such restaurants to serve permissible food to drunkards and sober customers alike? Is it a sin if that permissible food helps in decreasing the effect of intoxication or other similar effect?

Answer: On its merits, there is no problem in this.

273. Question: Is it permissible for a Muslim to sell **pork** to those who believe it is permissible for them like the Ahlul Kitāb?

Answer: It is not permissible to deal in pork at all.

274. Question: Is it permissible to work at a store that sells pork in the sense that the Muslim supervisor asks one of his employees to give pork to the customer?

Answer: It is not permissible to sell pork, even to those who consider it lawful, be it directly or through an intermediary.

As for handling pork to those who consider it lawful, there is problem in it; however, based on obligatory precaution, one should refrain from it.

275. Question: A person knows for sure that one day he will see a *harām* scene on television or video. Is it then permissible to buy it?

Answer: The reason compels him not to buy.

276. Question: You have said that a Muslim is allowed to buy **lottery** tickets if he intends to contribute to a charitable cause, i.e. with no intention of probable prize. Now, if a Muslim intends that he is donating some part of the price of the lottery ticket for a charitable cause that the lottery company chooses, and the rest of the price is with the intention of winning the prize—would it be permissible to buy the lottery ticket with such an intention?

Answer: It is not permissible.

277. Question: Is it allowed for a mature and responsible Muslim to encourage a child to buy a lottery ticket and then ask him to present it to himself as a gift? Is it permissible for him to ask an Ahlul Kitāb person to buy the ticket [for him] with the intention of winning the prize?

Answer: The prohibition is not lifted by any of those [loop holes] because the rule of causing or delegating [the act of buying the lottery ticket] is like doing it directly.

278. Question: Is it permissible to buy, say, honey, which has on it a lottery ticket with the intention of winning the probable prize at the time of buying?

Answer: It is permissible if the entire price is for the honey and not for the probable prize.

279. Question: A Muslim wins a lottery prize and then decides to donate a portion of the prize to a charitable organization. Is it permissible for that charitable organization to accept the money [or the item] and use it for the welfare of Muslims? And does it make a difference if the intention of the winner from the very beginning had been to use some of the prize for the well-being of Muslims?

Answer: If the prize belongs to those whose wealth is not sacrosanct [in Islam], it is permissible to utilize it.

280. Question: If a winner of the lottery performs hajj with the prize of the lottery, is his hajj valid?

Answer: The ruling is clear from the answer of the last question.

281. Question: If an unjust and usurping establishment gives an amount of money to a Muslim [and he spends it for hajj], what is the status of his hajj?

Answer: If it is not known that that particular money was aquired unlawfully, the recipient should not worry if the giver is unjust and usurper.

282. Question: Is it permissible **to work in a restaurant** where intoxicating drinks are served, if the worker does not himself serve them; nevertheless, sometimes he would be washing the cutlery [in which the drinks were served]?

Answer: If washing the cutlery used for intoxicating drinks is considered as a first step in drinking the liquor and serving it to the customers, it is forbidden.

283. Question: A Muslim who is committed to promote his religion is compelled to work in a governmental department in the West; this may lead to committing certain forbidden acts. He does this with the hope that he will have in future a greater influence in that department. In this way he serves his religion and considers this service more important than committing the past forbidden acts. Is this permissible for him?

Answer: It is not permissible to commit forbidden act just for future [positive] expectations.

284. Question: Is it permissible for a holder of law degree to become a **lawyer** in a non-Muslim country upholding the laws of that country, and taking cases of non-Muslims since his purpose is to attract cases irrespective of their nature?

Answer: If it does not involve violation of a right or lying or other forbidden acts, there is no problem in it.

285. Question: Is it permissible for a holder of law degree to become a judge in non-Muslim countries in which he acts according to their laws?

Answer: It is not permissible to administer judgement for those who are not qualified, and [it is not permissible to judge] based on non-Islamic laws.

286. Question: An electrical engineer in a European country is sometimes called to install or repair public address systems; at times those places are establishments for illicit entertainment. Is it permissible for him to engage in this work in such places with the knowledge that if he declines the customer, it will hurt his business, in that customers will eventually leave him?

Answer: It is permissible.

287. Question: A person works in a restaurant in which he might be required to serve meat that is not *halāl* or pork to non-Muslims. You have kindly answered the first situation; but the question remains with regard to the second situation that involves serving pork alongside the meat that is not *halāl*. Is this allowed? If he refuses to serve in this case, he might lose his job and be fired.

Answer: Serving pork even to those who consider it lawful is a problem; and based on obligatory precaution, it must be avoided.

288. Question: Is a Muslim allowed to work in grocery stores that sell liquor in one of its sections, and his work is only as a cashier?

Answer: He is allowed to receive the price of items other than liquor and also the price of liquor if the buyers are non-Muslims.

289. Question: A printer in the West prints the menu for a restaurants. Such menus include pork. Is this allowed? Is he allowed to print the advertisements for pubs and establishments that provide forbidden entertainment knowing well that his business will be affected if he does not print these kinds of materials?

Answer: It is not permissible for him to do that even if it affects his business.

* * *

Chapter Five

INTERACTION IN SOCIAL LIFE

Introduction

Each society has its own social circumstances with its own traditions, formalities, values and habits. It is natural that the values and customs of societies in foreign countries would differ from the values and habits of our Muslim societies. These differences place the Muslim living in such societies, in a constant state of questing about what is permissible for him and what is not.

Residing in societies that cater for Western values imposes upon the immigrants (from Muslim countries) the resistance against becoming absorbed in the melting pot of the new values, and the protection of themselves and their children from gradually melting into it. This is bound to put upon them extra hardship to protect themselves, their families and children from their destructive influences.

Therefore, it is better to explain the following religious laws.

General Rules

[Rights of one's Relatives]

290. Maintaining **ties with one's relations** *(silatur rahim)* is obligatory upon Muslims, and severing those ties *(qat'ur rahim)* is one of the major sins. Since maintaining the ties is obligatory and severing them is a major sin for which Allah has threatened Hell-fire, the need for maintaining the ties becomes more important in foreign lands; and observing this obligation takes greater priority in countries where relations are few, families break up, religious bonds erode, and material values rule supreme.

Allāh, the Almighty, has forbidden the severing of ties with one's relatives. He said in the Holy Book: *"But if you held command, you were sure to make mischief in the land and cut off the ties of kinship! Those it is whom Allāh has cursed so He has made them deaf and blinded their eyes."* (47:22)

Imam 'Ali (a.s.) said, "A family that is united and whose members support one another, Allāh gives them sustenance even if they be sinners; a family that is divided and severs ties with one another, Allāh deprives them [from sustenance] even if they be pious."[55]

It has been narrated from Imam al-Bāqir (a.s.) that: "In the book of 'Ali [it says], 'There are three traits whoever possesses them shall not die until he sees their evil consequences: adultery, severing the ties with one's relations, and a false oath in which Allāh is invoked. Indeed the good deed that expedites reward is maintaining the ties with one's relations. There could be a people who are sinners but they

---

[55] Al-Kulayni, *al-Usûl mina 'l-Kāfi*, vol. 2, p. 348.

maintain ties with one another, and so their wealth increases and they have affluence. Verily a false oath and severing of ties will destroy populated centres."[56]

291. It is harãm to sever the ties with one's relation even if that person had severed his ties [with you]. It is harãm to do so even if he or she is negligent of salãt, a drunkard, and takes some religious injunctions lightly (for example by not observing the *hijãb,* and etc) to an extent that there is no use in advising, counseling or warning him or her. This prohibition is only lifted when maintaining the ties encourages that relation to continue in his or her immoral ways.

Our holy Prophet Muhammad (s.a.w.) said, "The best of virtues is to maintain the ties with one who has severed it; to give in charity to one who has deprived you [of help]; and to forgive one who has done wrong to you."[57] He also said, "Do not sever the ties with your relations even if they have severed them with you."[58]

292. Probably the least of deeds that a Muslim can do (within the realm of possibility and ease) in order to maintain the ties with his relations is to visit them and meet them; or to inquire about their well being by enquiring even from far [via telephone, etc].

Our noble Prophet Muhammad (s.a.w.) said, "The good deed that brings rewards fastest [than other deeds] is maintaining the ties with one's relations."[59] Imam 'Ali (a.s.) said, "Maintain the link with your relations even by greeting. Allãh, the Almighty, says, *'Be careful of (your duty towards) Allãh by whom you demand of one another (your rights), and*

---

56   Ibid, p. 347.
57   An-Narãqi, *Jãmi'u 's-Sa'ãdãt,* vol. 2, p. 260.
58   Al-Kulayni, *al-Usûl mina 'l-Kãfi,* vol. 2, p. 347; also see as-Sadûq, *Man La Yahdhuruhu 'l-Faqíh,* vol. 4, p. 267.
59   Ibid, vol. 2, p. 152.

(to) the ties of relationship; surely Allāh ever watches over you.' (4:1)"[60]

Imam as-Sādiq (a.s.) said, "Maintaining the ties and charity make the accountability [of the Day of Judgement] simple, and protects from the sins. Therefore, maintain the ties with your relations and be charitable towards your brethren even by greeting kindly and replying to the greetings."[61]

[The Parents]

293. The most serious type of severing the ties is **causing distress (*'uqūq*) to the parents** whom Almighty Allāh has enjoined kindness and compassion. The Almighty says in His noble Book, *"And your Lord enjoins that you should not worship but Him and be kind to the parents. If either or both of them reach old age with you, say not to them (so much as) 'ugh' nor chide them, and speak to them a generous word."* (17:23)

The Imam says, "The lowest kind of *'uqūq* is to say 'ugh'. If Allāh the Almighty had known anything lower than that, He would surely have forbidden it."[62]

Imam as-Sādiq (a.s.) said, "Anyone who looks towards his parents with hatred even if they had been unjust to him, Allāh shall not accept his salāt." There are many such ahādíth.[63]

294. As opposed to the above is **being kind to one's parents** which indeed is the best means of attaining the pleasure of Almighty Allāh. He has said in the holy Qur'ān: *"...and lower for them the wings of humility out of mercy, and say, 'My Lord! Have mercy on them as they had nourished me when I was an infant.'"* (17:24)

[60] Ibid, vol. 2, p. 155.
[61] Ibid, vol. 2, p. 157.
[62] Ibid, vol. 2, p. 348.
[63] Ibid.

Ibrāhim bin Shuʻayb narrates that he said to Imam as-Sādiq (a.s.), "My father has become very old and weak to an extent that we carry him [to the toilet] when need be." He said, "If you can help him in that, then do so, and [also] feed him with your hand because this [service] will be a shield [against the hell-fire] for you tomorrow [i.e., in the next world]."[64]

Maintaining the ties with one's **mother before the father** has also been mentioned in many noble *ahādíth*. Imam as-Sādiq (a.s.) said, "A person came to the Prophet Muhammad (s.a.w.) and said, 'O Messenger of Allāh! To whom should I do a good deed?' He replied, 'To your mother.' Then the person asked, 'Then who?' The Prophet replied, 'Your mother.' Then the person asked, 'Then who?' The Prophet replied, 'Your mother.' Then the person asked, 'Then who?' The Prophet answered, 'Your father.'"[65] (See the question-answer section below.)

295. In some ahādíth the right of the **eldest brother** over the younger ones has been mentioned. This right should be observed and implemented in order to strengthen the ties of brotherhood within the single family and to guarantee its survival as a strong and well-knit structure if and when it goes through a rough patch. The Prophet Muhammad (s.a.w.) said, " The right of the eldest brother over the younger ones is like the right of the father over his child."[66]

296. Besides the guardian of the child or someone authorized by him, no one is allowed to physically **punish a child** when he commits a forbidden act or causes harm to others.

The guardian and someone authorized by him are allowed to discipline a child. [However, there are limits that must be

---

[64] Ibid, vol. 2, p. 162.
[65] Ibid, vol. 2, p. 160.
[66] An-Narāqi, *Jāmiʻu 's-Saʻādāt*, vol. 2, p. 267.

observed:] the act of, say, hitting should be light, not agonizing, and should not be such that it leaves bruises on the child's skin; that it should not exceed three hits [in one instance]; and that also only when disciplining the child depends on physically hitting him.

Therefore, the elder brother does not have a right to hit the younger brother unless he is the legal guardian of the child or authorized by the guardian.

It is not permissible at all to hit a school pupil without the permission of his guardians or someone authorized by the guardian. (See the question-answer section below.)

297. It is not permissible to hit a *bāligh* child in order to prevent him from an evil act, except in accordance with the conditions of *al-amru bi 'l-ma'rûf wa 'n-nahi 'ani 'l-munkar* (enjoining the good and forbidding the evil) with the permission of the religious authority. Based on obligatory precaution, a *bāligh* child should not be hit at all.

[The Elderly]

298. Respecting the Elders: The noble Prophet Muhammad (s.a.w.) has asked us to respect the elderly and honour them. He said, "One who recognizes the virtue of an elder person and honours him for his age, Allāh shall protect him from the fear of the Day of Judgement."[67] He also said, "One way of exalting Allāh, the Almighty, is to honour the believer with a white beard."[68]

[Visiting One Another]

299. Many noble ahādíth from the Prophet (s.a.w.) and the Imams (a.s.) have emphasized the idea of visiting one another, maintaining cordial relationship among the believers, making the believers happier, fulfilling their needs, visiting their sick, participating in their funerals, and helping them in good as

---

[67] As-Sadûq, *Thawābu 'l-A'māl wa 'Iqābu 'l-A'māl*, p. 225.
[68] Ibid.

well as restrained circumstances. Imam as-Sādiq (a.s.) said, "Anyone who visits his brother [in faith] for the sake of Allāh, Almighty Allāh will says, 'You have visited Me, therefore your reward is upon Me, and I will not be satisfied with a reward for you less than Paradise.'"[69]

The Imam said to Khaythamah, "Convey our greetings to those who love us and advise them to fear Allāh, and that the affluent and strong ones among them should visit the poor and weak ones, and they should participate in their funerals, and meet one another in their homes."[70]

[The Neighbour]

300. The right of the **neighbour** is close [in importance] to the right of kin. A Muslim one and a non-Muslim neighbour are equal in this right because the Messenger of Allāh (s.a.w.) established the right of the non-Muslim neighbour when he said: "There are three kinds of neighbours: 1. Some of them have three rights [upon you]: the right of Islam, the right of neighbourhood, and the right of relationship. 2. Some have two rights: the right of Islam and the right of neighbourhood. 3. Some have just one right: the non-Muslim who has the right of neighbourhood."[71]

The Prophet said, "The best neighbourly act is to be trustworthy for those who are your neighbours."[72]

In the advice Imam 'Ali gave to Imams al-Hasan and al-Husayn after the accursed Ibn Muljim had wounded him, he also talked about neighbours. He said, "be mindful of your

---

[69] Al-Kulayni, *al-Usûl mina 'l-Kāfi,* vol. 2, p. 176.

[70] Ibid; for more information, see the sections "Fulfilling the Needs of Believer" (vol. 2, p. 192), "Striving for Need of a Believer" (vol. 2, p. 196), "Relieving the Suffering of a Believer" (vol. 2, p. 199) of *al-Usûl mina 'l-Kāfi* of al-Kulayni.

[71] An-Nuri, *Mustadraku 'l-Wasā'il* ("Kitābu 'l-Hajj"), section 72.

[72] An-Narāqi, *Jāmi'u 's-Sa'ādāt,* vol. 2, p. 267. Also see the section on "rights of the neighbour" in *al-Usûl mina 'l-Kāfi,* vol. 2, p. 666.

duty towards Allāh regarding your neighbours because it was the advice of your Prophet who continuously advised about them until we thought that he might give them a share in our estate."[73]

Imam as-Sādiq (a.s.) said, "Accursed, accursed is he who harasses his neighbour."[74] He also said, "One who does not maintain good neighbourly relations with his neighbours is not one of us."[75] (See the question-answer section below.)

301. Among the qualities of the good believers is to emulate the noble character of Prophet Muhammad (a.s.) whom the Almighty has described in His book as following: *"And you verily are on high level of noble character."* (68: 4-6.)[76]

Indeed the Messenger of Allāh (s.a.w.) said, "Nothing will be placed on the scale of the Day of Judgement better than good character."[77] Once the Prophet was asked, "Who is the best in faith among the believers?" He replied, "The best among them in character."[78]

[Truthfulness]

302. Among the qualities of good believers is **truthfulness** in speech and action, and fulfilling the promise. Almighty Allāh has praised Prophet Ismā'īl (a.s.) by saying: *"He indeed was true in [fulfillment of] promise and was a messenger, a prophet."* (19:54) The noble Prophet said, "One who believes

---

[73] *Nahju 'l-Balāgha* (ed. Subhi as-Sālih) p. 422.

[74] *Mustadraku 'l-Wasā'il,* vol. 1, section 72.

[75] An-Narāqi, *Jāmi'u 's-Sa'ādāt,* vol. 2, p. 268.

[76] To know more about the noble character of the Prophet (a.s.), see at-Tabrasi, *Makārimu 'l-Akhlāq,* p. 15ff, and the various books of history and hadíth.

[77] An-Narāqi, *Jāmi'u 's-Sa'ādāt,* vol. 1, p. 443.

[78] Ibid, vol. 2, p. 331. Also see *al-Usûl mina 'l-Kāfi,* vol. 2, p. 99 and *Wasā'ilu 'sh-Shí'a,* vol. 15, p. 198ff.

in Allāh and the Last Day should fulfill whatever he promises."[79]

The importance of truthfulness and fulfillment of promise is more emphasized clear when we realize that many non-Muslims judge Islam by the action of Muslims. As much good a Muslim does, he positively portrays Islam to non-Muslims through his good conduct, and as much evil a Muslim does, he negatively portrays Islam through his bad conduct.

[Husand and Wife]

303. Among the qualities of a **good wife** is refraining from harassing, hurting, and irritating her husband. Among the qualities of a **good husband** is refraining from harassing, hurting, and irritating his wife. The Prophet (s.a.w.) said, "If a man has a wife who harasses him, Allāh will neither accept her ritual prayer *(salāt)* nor any of her good deeds —until she has pleased him— even if she fasts and prays at all times, emancipates slaves, and gives away her wealth in charity for the sake of Allāh. She will be the first to enter the Fire." Then he said, "And the husband has the same burden and chastisement if he is a harasser and unjust [in his behaviour towards his wife]."[80]

[Friendship with non-Muslims]

304. A Muslim is allowed to take **non-Muslims for acquaintances and friends**, to be sincere towards them and they be sincere towards him, to help them and they help him in fulfilling the needs of this life. Almighty Allāh has said in His noble Book: *"Allāh does not forbid you in regard to those who have not made war against you on account of (your) religion, and have not driven you forth from your homes, that you show them kindness and deal with them justly; surely Allāh loves the doers of justice."* (60:8)

---

[79] An-Narāqi, ibid. Also see *al-Usûl mina 'l-Kāfi,* vol. 2, p. 363ff.
[80] Al-Hurr al-'Āmili, *Wasā'ilu 'sh-Shi'a,* vol. 20, p. 82. Also see 'Abdu 'l-Husayn Dastghayb, *adh-Dhunûbu 'l-Kabírah,* vol. 2, p. 296-297.

When these kinds of friendship produce good results, it guarantees that the non-Muslim friend, neighbour, or colleague and business partner will know about the values of Islam, and it will bring him closer to this upright religion. The Prophet said to Imam 'Ali, "If Allãh guides through you a single person from His servants, that is better for you than anything upon which the Sun shines from the east to the west."[81] (See the question-answer section below.)

305. It is permissible to greet Ahlul Kitãb (the Jews and the Christians, etc) and also the non-Ahlul Kitãb on the occasions they celebrate like the New Year, Christmas, Easter, and the Passover.

[*Al-Amr bi 'l-Ma'rûf* and *an-Nahi 'ani 'l-Munkar*]

306. Enjoining good and forbidding evil are obligatory rituals, whenever the conditions exist, on all believing men and women. Almighty Allãh has said in His noble Book: *"There should be a group from among you who should be calling (people) to the good, enjoining the good, and forbidding the evil; they are the successful ones."* (3:104) He also said, *"The believing men and the believing women are helpers of one another, they enjoin the good and forbid the evil."* (9:71)

Our noble Prophet Muhammad (s.a.w.) said, "My community will continue to be blessed as long they enjoin the good and forbid the evil, and help one another in good deeds. When they do not do this, blessings will be withheld from them, and some [evil persons] among them will have hegemony over the others; and they shall have no helper neither on the earth nor in the heaven."[82]

---

[81] An-Nuri, *Mustadraku 'l-Wasã'il,* vol. 12, p. 241.

[82] Al-Hurr al-'Ãmili, *Wasã'ilu 'sh-Shi'a,* vol. 16, p. 396.

Imam Ja'far as-Sādiq (a.s.) narrates from the Messenger of Allāh (s.a.w.) who said, "How will it be with you when your women will become corrupt and, your youths sinful while you will not be enjoining the good nor forbidding the evil?" The people said, "Will this happen, O the Messenger of Allāh?" He replied, "Yes; and even worse than that. How will it be with you when you will be enjoining the evil and forbidding the good?" The people said, "O Messenger of Allāh, will this actually happen?" He said, "Yes, and even worse than that. How will it be with you when you will think of good as evil and of evil as good?"[83]

These two obligations become more pressing when the person neglecting the good or committing the evil is one of your family members. You might find someone among your family who neglects some obligations or takes them lightly; you might find some of them performing *wudhu* or *tayammum* or *ghusl* incorrectly, or does not purify his body and clothes from impurities correctly. Or does not recite the two *surahs* and the obligatory recitations in *salāt* correctly; or does not purify his wealth by paying *khums* and *zakāt*.

You might find someone among your family members committing some sins like masturbation or gambling or listening to songs or drinking intoxicants or eating *harām* meat or devouring people's property unlawfully or cheating and stealing.

You might find someone among the women in your family not observing *hijāb*, not concealing her hair; and you might find that she does not remove the nail polish at the time of *wudhu* or *ghusl*. You might even find among them someone who wears perfume for men other than her husband; and does not conceal her hair or body from the eyes of her cousins (maternal or paternal) and of her brother-in-law or husband's

---

[83] Ibid, vol. 16, p. 122.

friend with the justification that they all live in the same house, under the pretext that he is like her brother, or other similar groundless excuses.

You might find someone in your family who habitually lies, backbites and infringes upon the rights of others, usurps people's property, supports the wrong-doers in their unjust activities, and harasses his neighbour, etc.

If you find any such situations, you should enjoin the good and forbid the evil by applying the first two methods: that is, expressing your displeasure at the situation, and then speaking about it. If these two methods do not work, then apply the third method (after asking the permission from the *mujtahid*): adopting practical [or physical] measures moving from softer to harsher ones.

If that person is ignorant of the religious rules, it is your duty to teach them, if they have the intention of learning and acting accordingly.

[Kindness towards People]

307. Kindness towards people, all the people, is among recommended rituals that have been emphasized by our religion. The Messenger of Allāh said, "My Lord has commanded me to be kind towards the people just as He has commanded me to fulfill the obligatory [prayers]." He also said, "If a person does not have three things, his deeds are not complete: [spiritual] armor that prevents him from disobeying Allāh; noble character by which he shows kindness towards the people; and patience by which he repels the foolishness of the ignorant person."[84]

Kindness is not limited to the Muslims only. It has been narrated that Imam 'Ali (a.s.) became a travelling companion of a non-Muslim on the way to Kufa. When they reached to a

---

[84] *Wasā'ilu 'sh-Shi'a*, vol. 12, p. 200.

crossroad the non-Muslims, the Imam walked with him for a distance before saying farewell. The non-Muslim asked him why he walked that extra distance, the Imam replied, "This is the right of companionship, i.e. see them through for a short distance when they separate. This is what our Prophet has ordered us to do."[85] That man accepted Islam because of this noble character.

An interesting story was narrated by ash-Sha'bi concerning the justice of Imam 'Ali with one of his non-Muslim subjects. He narrates that one day 'Ali bin Abi Tālib went to the market and saw a Christian selling a coat of arms. 'Ali (a.s.) recognized that coat of arms and said to the seller that, "This is my body of armour; let us go to the judge of the Muslims." The Muslim judge was Shurayh, and 'Ali himself had appointed him in that position.

When they went to Shurayh, he said, "What is the matter, O Amiru 'l-mu'mineen?" 'Ali (a.s.) said, "This is my coat of arms which I had lost since a long time now." Then Shurayh asked the seller, "O Christian, what do you have to say?" The Christian seller said, "I am not accusing Amiru 'l-mu'mineen of lying, but the coat of arms is my property." So Shurayh turned to 'Ali (a.s.) and said, "I do not see [any ground on which] you can take it from his possession. Do you have a proof [supporting your claim]?" Since 'Ali (a.s.) had no proof, he said, "Shurayh is correct [in his judgement]."[86]

On hearing the judgement, the Christian seller said, "I bear witness that these are the laws of the prophets: the Leader of the Believers comes to a judge appointed by himself, and the

---

[85] Ibid, p. 135.
[86] Translator's Note: Shurayh's judgement was based on the principle that possession is itself a proof of ownership, and that the claimant has to provide the proof in support of his claim.

judge passes a judgement against him! By God, O Amiru 'l-mu'mineen, this coat of arms is yours—I followed you in the army, and the coat of arms slipped down from your camel, so I took it. I bear witness that there is no god but Allāh and that Muhammad is the Messenger of Allāh." 'Ali (a.s.) said, "Now that you have become a Muslim, it belongs to you." Then he carried it on a horse. Sha'bi says that he subsequently saw that Christian fighting the non-Muslims. This version of the hadíth has been narrated from Abu Zakariyya.[87]

Similarly, we have heard from Amiru 'l-mu'mineen 'Ali (a.s.) what could be considered as a historical precedence of social security that is so commonly practiced at present in the Western world. 'Ali did not differentiate between a Muslim and a non-Muslim in the Islamic state. The narrator says that one day an old blind person passed by him begging. Imam 'Ali (a.s.), "What is this?" Those who were around him said, "O Amiru 'l-mu'mineen, he is a Christian!" Imam 'Ali (a.s.) answered, "You have used him until he became old and incapable, and now you are depriving him [of the benefits]! Provide for him from the public treasury."[88]

It has also been narrated from Imam as-Sādiq (a.s.), "If a Jewish person comes to sit with you, make that a good meeting."[89]

[Making Peace between People]

308. There is a great reward in **making peace between people,** reconciling their differences, making them friends of one another, and lessening the gulf of disagreement between them. More so when making peace is done in a non-Muslim

---

[87] As-Sayyid al-Milāni in *Qādatunā,* quoting al-Bayhaqi, *as-Sunanu 'l-Kubra,* vol. 4, p. 135.

[88] At-Tusi, *at-Tahdhib,* vol. 6, p. 292.

[89] *Wasā'ilu 'sh-Shí'a,* vol. 12, p. 201.

land far away from the homeland, family, relations, and friends. Imam 'Ali (a.s.) had given certain advice to his sons, al-Hassan and al-Husayn, just before his death after the Kharijite Ibn Muljim al-Murādi had injured him. He said, "I advise you both, all my children and family members, and whosoever to whom this letter of mine reaches: to fear Allāh, to organize your affairs, to establish peace because I have heard your grandfather (s.a.w.) say, 'Making peace is better than a whole year of praying and fasting.'"[90]

[Sincere Advice for Muslim Brethren]

309. Sincere advice —that is, to wish that the blessings of Allāh may continue on the believing brethren, to dislike that evil may afflict them, and to exert efforts in guiding them towards what is good for them— is among the deeds loved by the Almighty Allāh.

There are countless ahādíth on the importance of sincere advice. For instance, the Prophet (s.a.w.) said, "The person with greatest status in the eyes of Allāh on the Day of Judgement will be the person who worked most in His earth to give sincere councel to His creatures."[91] Imam al-Bāqir (a.s.) said, "The Messenger of Allāh (s.a.w.) said, 'A person from among you should give sincere advice to his brother in faith as if he is advising himself.'"[92] Imam as-Sādiq (a.s.) said, "It is necessary for a believer to sincerely advise another believer in presence as well as in absence."[93] He also said, "You should be careful about advising Allāh's creatures sincerely for His sake because you can never meet Allāh with a deed better than that."[94]

---

[90] *Nahju 'l-Balāgha* (Subhi as-Sālih's edition) p. 421.
[91] *Al-Usûl mina 'l-Kāfi,* vol. 2, p. 208.
[92] Ibid; also see *Jāmi'u 's-Sa'ādāt,* vol. 2, p. 213.
[93] Ibid.
[94] Ibid, vol. 2, p. 164; for more information see the relevent sections in *Wasā'ilu 'sh-Shi'a,* vol. 16, p. 381-384.

[Spying]

310. Spying —that is, snooping in order to gain information and embarrass people— is forbidden in Islamic laws. Almighty Allāh has said in His book: *"O You who believe, refrain from most of suspicions because some suspicions are sins, and do not spy..."* (49:12)

Ishāq bin 'Ammār, a companion of Imam as-Sādiq (a.s.), said: I heard as-Sādiq (a.s.) saying, "The Messenger of Allāh (s.a.w.) said, 'O you who have accepted Islam with your tongue [i.e., with your verbal declarations of faith] and faith is yet to enter your hearts! Do not disparage the Muslims nor disclose their frailties because whosoever discloses their shortcomings, Allāh shall disclose his; and he whose weaknesses are disclosed by Allāh, will indeed be disgraced, even if he is inside his house.'"[95]

[Backbiting, *Namímah*]

311. Backbiting means "speaking ill of a believer in their absence with the purpose of disparaging or not, and no matter whether the alleged shortcoming was related to his body, his lineage, his behaviour, his deeds, his statements, his religion, or his life, and other defects which are [usually] concealed from the people. Similarly, it does not matter whether the description was done by words or by gesture."[96]

Almighty Allāh has condemned backbiting in His noble Book and has described it such that mind and body feel abhorrence towards it. He said, *"And some of you should not backbite the others: would anyone of you like to eat the flesh of his dead brother? No, you abhor it."* (49:12)

The Prophet (s.a.w.) said, "Be careful of backbiting because backbiting is worse than adultery, in that a person

---

95 Ibid, vol. 12, p. 275.
96 As-Sayyid as-Sistāni, *Minhāju 's-Sāliheen*, vol. 1, p. 17.

who commits adultery can repent and ask forgiveness from God, and Allāh can forgive him whereas, Allāh will not forgive the backbiter until the person who was at the receiving end forgives him."[97]

It is not appropriate for a believer to listen to backbiting against his believing brother. Indeed it appears from the sayings of the Prophet and the Imams (may Allāh bless them all) that it is obligatory upon one who hears backbiting to support the person who is being disparaged; and that if he does not repel the backbiting [against his believing brother], Allāh will abandon him in this world as well as in the hereafter, and he shall be held accountable just like the one who backbited.

312. When we talk about backbiting, another religious terminology also comes to the mind of the believer that has been equally forbidden by Islam for the sake of holding the society together. It is the term known as *"an-namímah"* which means sowing dissension by statements like "So and so was saying this and that about you" with the intention of damaging the relationship between the believers or increasing bitterness between them.

The Messenger of Allāh (s.a.w.) has said, "Shall I not inform you of the worst person among you?" People said, "Yes, O Messenger of Allāh!" He said, "Those who spread slanderous rumours; those who divide friends."[98] Imam al-Bāqir (a.s.) said, "The Paradise is forbidden upon the backbiters and those who spread slanderous rumours."[99] Similarly, Imam as-Sādiq (a.s.) said, "The spiller of blood [i.e., murderer], the one addicted to intoxicants, and one who spreads slanderous rumours will not enter Paradise."[100]

---

[97] An-Narāqi, *Jāmi'u 's-Sa'ādāt*, vol. 2, p. 302.
[98] An-Narāqi, *Jāmi'u 's-Sa'ādāt*, vol. 2, p. 276.
[99] *Al-Usûl mina 'l-Kāfi*, vol. 2, p. 369.
[100] As-Sadûq, *Thawābu 'l-A'māl*, p. 262.

313. Suspicion. Almighty Allāh has forbidden us from having suspicious thoughts. He says in His noble Book, *"O you who believe! Refrain from most of the suspicions because some suspicions are a sin."* (49:12)

Based on this noble Qur'ānic verse, it is not permissible for a believer to entertain suspicious thoughts about his fellow Muslim without any clear proof and evidence because no one other than Allāh knows the inner-most thoughts of a person. So as long as it is possible to place the action of a believer in a proper context, we should do so until it is proven otherwise. Imam 'Ali (a.s.) said, "Place the affair of your brother in the best possible [context] until you get a proof which convinces you [of the contrary]. And do not have suspicious thoughts about a word that comes out of your brother [in faith] while you have a positive context for it."[101]

[Extravagance and Waste]

314. Extravagance and waste are two traits condemned by Almighty Allāh. He says, *"Eat and drink but do not waste because He does not like those who do the wastage."* (7:31) He has also condemned those who engage in waste by saying, *"Verily the wastrels are brethren of the Satans, and verily the Satan was ungrateful to his Lord."* (19:27)

Imam 'Ali (a.s.) wrote a letter to Ziyād in which he condemned wastage and squandering. He wrote: "Give up lavishness and be moderate. Every day remember the coming day. Hold back from the funds what you need and send forward the balance for the day of your need. Do you expect that Allāh may give you the reward of the humble while you yourself are arrogant in His view? And do you covet that He may give you the reward of those doing charity while you enjoy comforts and deny them to the weak and the widows?

---

[101] *Wasā'ilu 'sh-Shī'a*, vol. 8, chapter 161.

Certainly, a man is rewarded according to what he has done, and he shall meet what he has sent forward."[102]

[Charity]

315. Charity for the sake of Allāh: Allāh has encouraged us in His noble Book to give charity for His sake and has described it as a deal which will never go sour. He says, *"Those who recite the Book of Allāh, establish the prayer, and give in charity secretly as well as openly out of what We have given them, they hope for a deal that will never go sour. Allāh shall pay them their rewards in full and give them more out of His grace; indeed He is Forgiving, Multiplier of rewards."* (35:29-30) In another chapter, He says, *"Who is there that will offer to Allāh a good loan so that He will double it for him, and he shall have an excellent reward. On that day you will see the believing men and the believing women while their light shall be running before them and on their right side— [they will be told:] 'good news to you today: gardens beneath which rivers flow, to abide therein, that is the great achievement.'"* (57:11-12)

In a third verse, Allāh reminds us to hasten to giving charity before death approaches us. He says, *"And give in charity out of what We have given you before death comes to one of you, so that he should say, 'My Lord! Why did Thou not respite me to a near term, so that I should have given alms and been of the doers of good deeds?' And Allāh does not respite a soul when its appointed term has come, and Allāh is Aware of what you do."* (63:10-11)

Then Allāh clarifies the end of those who hoard wealth and do not spend in charity for His sake. He says, *"(As for) those who hoard up gold and silver and do not spend it in Allāh's way, announce to them a painful chastisement on the day when it shall be heated in the fire of hell, then their foreheads and their sides and their backs shall be branded with it; this is*

---

[102] *Nahju 'l-Balāgha*, letter no. 21.

what you hoarded up for yourselves, therefore taste what you hoarded." (9:34-35)

Imam 'Ali (a.s.) was the living example and the embodiment of the great values of Islam; he gave in charity whatever his hands could hold, preferring frugality in this transitory world and avoiding its beauties and luxuries while he had the control of the entire public treasury of the Muslims. He describes himself [in the letter to his governor in Basra] as follows:

"If I wished I could have taken the way leading towards (worldly pleasures like) pure honey, fine wheat and silk clothes but it cannot be that my passions lead me and greed takes me to choosing good meals while there may be people in the Hijaz and in Yamāmah who have no hope of getting bread or who do not have a full meal. Shall I lie with a full belly while around me there may be hungry bellies and thirsty livers? Or shall I be as the poet has said,

It is enough for you to have a disease
that you lie with your belly full
While around you people may be badly yearning
for dried meat?"[103]

Various sayings have come from the Prophet Muhammad (s.a.w.) and the Imams (a.s.) describing clearly the outcome of and benefits gained by the person who gives in charity, not only in this world, but also more than what he expects on *"the day when neither wealth shall benefit [a person] nor children."*

Sustenance is one reward that a generous person gets. The Prophet (s.a.w.) said, "Let sustenance flow [from God] through charity."[104] Curing disease is another benefit of giving

---

[103] *Nahju 'l-Balāghah*, letter no. 45.
[104] Al-Majlisi, *Bihāru 'l-Anwār*, vol. 19, p. 118.

charity. The Prophet (s.a.w.) said, "Cure your sick ones through charity."[105] Prolonging life span and averting tragic death is another result of giving charity. Imam al-Bāqir (a.s.) said, "Benevolence and charity eliminate poverty, prolong life span, and spare the charitable person seventy kinds of tragic deaths."[106] Fulfillment of debts and [increase in] blessings are also benefits of giving in charity. Imam as-Sādiq (a.s.) said, "Charity fulfills the payments of debts and yields."[107] The children of a charitable person are taken care of after his death. Imam as-Sādiq (a.s.) said, "No person has given good charity in this world but that Allāh has made good provision for his children after him."[108]

Imam al-Bāqir (a.s.) said, "If I could take care of a Muslim family, feeding the hungry among them, giving clothes to the naked among them, and protecting their honour in society [by them not having to beg], this is preferable than going for hajj, [then another] hajj, [then a third] hajj until I go ten times or even until I go seventy times."[109]

Giving charity for the sake of Allāh is a vast subject that cannot be fully covered in this short treatise.[110]

[Gifts for Family members]

316. The Messenger of Allāh (s.a.w.) had encouraged heads of family to buy **gifts for their families so as to make them happy.** Ibn 'Abbās narrates from the Messenger of Allāh (s.a.w.) that he said, "Whosoever enters a market and buys a

---

105 Al-Himyari, *Qurbu 'l-Asnād,* p. 74.
106 As-Sadûq, *al-Khisāl,* vol. 1, p. 25.
107 *Wasā'lu 'sh-Shi'a,* vol. 6, p. 255.
108 Ibid, vol. 19, p. 118.
109 As-Sadûq, *Thawābu 'l-A'māl,* p. 172.
110 For more information on this, see as-Sayyid 'Izzu 'd-Din Bahru 'l-'Ulûm, *al-Infāq fi Sabílillāh.*

gift, and takes it to his family is like a person who takes charity to those who are in need of it."[111]

[Concern for the Muslim Ummah]

317. One of the issues that the Islamic *shari'a* has emphasized is the issue of **being concerned for the affairs of Muslims.** The Messenger of Allāh (s.a.w.) said, "Whosoever get up in the morning and has no concern for the affairs of Muslims is not a Muslim."[112] He also said, "Whosoever gets up without being concerned about the affairs of Muslims is not one of them."[113]

There are many other sayings on this issue which space does not allow to be mentioned here.[114]

Questions and Answers

318. Question: Is it permissible to participate in the **funeral** ceremony **of a non-Muslim** if he was, for example, a neighbour?

Answer: If the deceased and those organizing the funeral are not known to have hatred towards Islam and Muslims, there is no problem in participating in the funeral. However, it is better to walk behind the coffin and not in front of it.

319. Question: Is it permissible to exchange greetings and gifts with a non-Muslim if he is a neighbour or a co-worker, etc.?

---

[111] As-Sadûq, *Thawābu 'l-A'māl*, p. 239
[112] *Jāmi'u 's-Sa'ādāt*, vol. 2, p. 229.
[113] Ibid.
[114] See *al-Usûl mina 'l-Kāfī*, section on "Being Concerned for Affairs of the Muslims."

Answer: If he does not express hatred towards Islam and Muslims in words or actions, there is no problem in doing what is required in friendship like being good and charitable towards him. Almighty Allāh has said, *"Allāh does not forbid you in regard to those who have not made war against you on account of (your) religion, and have not driven you forth from your homes, that you show them kindness and deal with them justly; surely Allāh loves the doers of justice."* [60:8]

320. Question: Is it permissible for the people of Ahlul Kitāb and other **non-Muslims to enter the mosques** *(masjid)* and other Islamic places of worship [like husayniyya or imambargah which are not *masjid*]? And is it necessarily for us to enforce the *hijāb* on those [non-Muslim women] who do not observe *hijāb* and allow them to enter [the mosque or places of worship], if it is permissible?

Answer: Based on obligatory precaution, it is not permissible for them [i.e., non-Muslims] to enter the mosque *(masjid)*. As for them entering the places of worship and etc, there is no problem in it. If their entry [in imambargah or a husayniyya or a center] without *hijāb* is considered as a sign of disrespect, *hijāb* should be enforced on the [non-Muslim] women.

321. Question: Is it permissible to harass a Jewish or a Christian or an Atheist neighbour?

Answer: It is not permissible to harass them without justification.

322. Question: Is it permissible to give charity to the poor among non-Muslims? Would a person get reward [*thawāb* from Allāh] for this charity?

Answer: There is no problem in giving charity to [a non-Muslim] who does not display hatred against Islam and Muslims; and one who gives such a charity will be rewarded for this deed.

323. Question: Is it obligatory to enjoin the good *(amr bi 'l-ma'rûf)* and to forbid the evil *(nahi 'ani 'l-munkar)* in regard to those who are not followers of Islam or are from the Ahlul Kitāb who are receptive, without any harm coming our way?

Answer: Yes, it is obligatory, provided that the other conditions also exist. One of those other conditions is that the person to be admonished should not have an excuse for doing the evil or neglecting the obligation.

Being ignorant out of negligence is not an acceptable excuse; so such a person should first be guided to the right conduct, and then if he does not act accordingly, he should be asked to do good or be forbidden from doing evil.

However, if the evil deed is of a category that one knows Allāh does not like it to happen under any circumstances — like creating corruption in the earth, killing an innocent person, etc— it is necessary to prevent it even if the doer is ignorant out of innocence.

324. Question: In European schools, there are teachers who do not believe in any religion and reject the idea of God in front of their pupils. Is it permissible for Muslim pupils to remain in such schools knowing that they can be greatly influenced by their teachers?

Answer: It is not permissible; and the guardian of the child is fully responsible for that.

325. Question: Is it permissible for male and female students in elementary and secondary schools to mix when one knows that this mixing will surely lead one day to a forbidden act by the male or the female student, even if that is just [as minor an act as] a forbidden glance?

Answer: It is not permissible under the circumstances described [in the question].

326. Question: Is it permissible for a Muslim man to go to a mixed swimming pool with the knowledge that the women there are in their most indecent form and would not listen to any admonishing?

Answer: Although looking without bad thoughts or without lustful intentions at the women who are indecently dressed (and who would not listen to you if you wish to admonish them) is allowed, but based on obligatory precaution, going to such indecent places is absolutely forbidden.

327. Question: Is it permissible for those who reside in the West to send their *muhajjaba* daughters to co-ed schools (no matter whether education is compulsory or not) while there exist non co-ed schools which obviously are expensive or far or of low academic standard?

Answer: It is not permissible [even] if it [just] corrupts their character let alone if it harms their beliefs and their commitment to the faith which is what normally happens!

328. Question: Is it permissible for a Muslim youth to accompany the girls who study with him in foreign universities for walking together, in vacation tours and etc.?

Answer: It is not permissible except with surety that he will not get into a forbidden act.

329. Question: Is it permissible to look at a passionate scene taking place on the street?

Answer: It is not permissible to look at it with lustful intentions or with ill thoughts; rather, based on obligatory precaution, one should refrain from watching it totally.

330. Question: Is it permissible to go to a mixed [i.e., co-ed] cinema and other *harām* places of entertainment without having any confidence that one will not engage in a forbidden act?

Answer: It is not permissible.

331. Question: Is it permissible to swim in a mixed swimming pool without having any lustful intention in swimming?

Answer: Based on obligatory precaution, it is not permissible to go to the places of indecency at all.

332. Question: Is it permissible to go to sea beaches and public parks during sunny days for walking while one might come across scenes which are against the norm of decency?

Answer: Without a guarantee that one will not get into a forbidden act, it is not permissible.

333. Question: In European countries, public baths are built with certain considerations. Whether or not it is in direction of *qibla* is not one of their consideration unlike the situation in Muslim countries.

[1] Is it permissible for us to use such facilities while we do not know where the direction of the *qibla* is? [2] And if we know the baths face the direction of the *qibla,* is it permissible for us to use them? If it is not permissible, what is the solution?

Answer: [1] In the first case, based on obligatory precaution, it is not permissible to use them except after failing to know the direction of the *qibla* and that it is not possible to wait or that waiting would entail harm and place the person in difficulty.

[2] In the second case, based on obligatory precaution, it is necessary —while using the bathroom— to refrain from facing the *qibla* or turning one's back to it.

However, in the event of emergency, one should sit with their back towards the *qibla.* This is based on obligatory precaution.

334. Question: A Muslim residing in a non-Muslim countries finds a suitcase (full of clothes) with or without the owner's nametag on it. What should he do with it?

Answer: Suitcase of personal belongings normally has the nametag through which the owner can be contacted. If he knows that it belongs to a Muslim or a non-Muslim whose property is sacrosanct (or even if there is a likelihood —a considerable likelihood— [that it belongs to a non-Muslim whose property is sacrosanct]), it is necessary for him to announce for one whole year that he has found that item [so that the owner can come forward and claim it]. If he cannot find the owner [even after announcing for one year], he should, based on obligatory precaution, give it in charity.

However, if he knows that it belongs to a non-Muslim or others like them, it is permissible for him to take its possession provided he is not legally bound to announce what he finds in that country or to hand it over to the authorities, etc.[115] In the latter case, he is not allowed to take possession of it; rather it is compulsory for him to act in accordance with the legal undertaking.

335. Question: If I find an item in a European country without any distinctive sign on it [identifying the owner], is it permissible for me to take its possession?

Answer: If it has no distinctive sign by which it could be possible to contact the owner, it is permissible for you to take its possession except in the case [of the legal undertaking] that was mentioned earlier.

336. Question: Some people, be they Muslim or non-Muslim, in the West approach you with expensive items for sale at a price so cheap that the customer is almost convinced that the item is stolen. Is it permissible to buy it if one knows for sure or senses strong probability that it is an item stolen from a Muslim?

---

[115] Translator's Note: Agreement, in the above context, means "the immigration agreement made between the host country and the immigrant."

Answer: If one knows or gets a strong feeling that the item has been stolen from a person whose property is sacrosanct it is not permissible to buy it or take its possession.

337. Question: The price of cigarettes is very high in Western countries. Would it be forbidden to buy them because of extravagance and waste, especially when one knows that they are harmful [to one's health]?

Answer: It is permissible to buy them; and using them would not become harām for the reasons mentioned [in the question].

Of course, if **smoking** causes great harm to the smoker while there is no harm to him from quitting, or that quitting involves lesser harm, it is necessary for him to refrain from it.

338. Question: There are machines that can record the telephone conversations without the knowledge of the speaker. Is it permissible to record the voice of anyone without his knowledge in order to use it against them when the need arises?

Answer: It is not obligatory on one speaker to ask the permission of the other speaker to record the conversation on the telephone line. However, he is not allowed to publicize it or let others listen to it if it will cause an insult of a mo'min or disclose his secret — unless that is over-ridden by another equal or more important obligation.

339. Question: A photographer is asked to take pictures at a wedding reception where intoxicating drinks are served. Is this permissible for him?

Answer: It is not permissible to take pictures of the scenes of drinking intoxicants and other forbidden substances.

340. Question: What are the limits of obeying one's parents?

Answer: The duty of a child towards his parents is of two kinds:

The First: To be kind towards them by providing for them if they are in need. To provide for their day-to-day needs. To respond to their requests that are related to their daily lives at a level that is normal and usual for a human being in the sense that if he refuses to fulfill them it would be counted as "not being good to them" — and that would differ depending on whether they are healthy and strong or ill and weak.

The Second: To behave with them kindly by not offending them in word or action, even if they are unjust to him. In some religious text, it says, "And if they hit you, do not shun them; instead say, 'May Allāh forgive you.'"

This is as far as it relates to the parents' situation.

As for those issues concerning the affairs of the child himself by which he could offend one of the parents, these are of two kinds:

The First: If the parent's distress results from his concern for the child, it is forbidden for the child to do something that would cause the distress to his parent, no matter whether the parent has prevented him from it or not.

The Second: If the parent's distress results from of his own evil characteristics (for example, dislike for the good of this world or the hereafter for his child), this kind of distress has no bearing on the child and it is not obligatory upon the child to submit to the parents desires of this kind.

It becomes clear from this that, on its own, obeying the parents in their personal commands is not obligatory. And Allāh knows the best.

341. Question: Some parents fear for their children in the matter of enjoining the good and forbidding the evil [and, therefore, ask them not to do *amr* or *nahi*]. So, is it obligatory to obey them in this matter while the child knows that his advice will be effective and there is no danger to him [in doing *amr* or *nahi*]?

Answer: When it becomes obligatory upon the child [to do *amr* or *nahi*], with all the conditions, there can be no obedience to the created in disobeying the Creator.

342. Question: A son argues with his father or a daughter argues with her mother in a serious day-to-day issue in a heated manner that causes distress to the parents. Is this permissible for the children, and what is the limit when a child is not allowed to argue with the parent?

Answer: A child is allowed to discuss with the parents in matters that he or she thinks is not right; but the child must observe politeness and respect in the discussion; he or she should not angrily look at them nor raise his voice over theirs, let alone use harsh words and expressions.

343. Question: If a mother orders her son to divorce his wife with whom she has differences, is it obligatory upon him to obey her in this matter? What if she says, "You are an *'āq* child[116] if you do not divorce her"?

Answer: It is not obligatory for him to obey her in this matter, and her statement [about him becoming disobedient] has no effect whatsoever. Of course, as mentioned earlier, it is necessary for him to refrain from any insulting statement or action towards her.

344. Question: A father hits his child severely that it leaves blue or red marks on the skin—is it obligatory upon the father to pay the indemnity for bodily injury? Is the rule different if the person who hit the child was other than his father?

Answer: The indemnity is obligatory upon the one who hits [in the way described above] irrespective of whether he is the father or someone else.

---

[116] *'Āq* means a child who is disobedient to his parents.

345. Question: If a Muslim is sure of his father's displeasure —although he has not heard him say no— in him travelling abroad, then is it permissible for him to travel, if he knows that the journey is good for him?

Answer: If being kind towards the father —in the context mentioned earlier in the answer to a previous question— demands that the son should be close to him or that the father will be in distress out of his concern for the son, he should abstain from travelling as long as he will not be in loss; otherwise, it is not necessary for him to abstain [from travelling].

346. Question: Is it part of righteousness for the wife to serve the father, the mother, the brother and the sister of her husband? Is it part of kindness for the husband to be considerate of the father, the mother, the brother and the sister of his wife, especially in foreign countries?

Answer: There is not doubt it is part of righteousness and an example of kindness towards the husband or the wife; but it is not obligatory [upon them].

* * *

Chapter Six

MEDICAL ISSUES

Introduction

Because of the scientific and technological advancement in the West, the visit of Muslims to these countries for seeking treatment is increasing; just as the Muslim residents in these parts of the world need medical treatment as dictated by their health demands.

General Rules

347. It is not permissible to perform autopsy on the body of a dead Muslim for the sake of education and other purposes. It is only permissible if the life of another Muslim depends on it—even if in the future.

348. It is permissible to transplant an organ from an animal (even dogs and pigs) to a human being; the transplanted organ will be considered as an organ of the recipient; all rules will apply to it. So *salāt* will be permissible with it by considering it ritually pure *(tāhir)* after it becomes part of the human body and its cells become rejuvenated. (See the question-answer section below.)

349. It is not permissible for a doctor to switch off medical apparatus providing a Muslim patient with oxygen, even if he is brain dead, i.e. in vegetative state. This is because human life in Islam is sacrosanct.

The doctor should not give in to the demand of the patient or his family-members for stopping the medical aid. If the doctor pulls out the plug and the Muslim patient dies because of it, he will be considered killer.

350. It is not permissible for a medical student to look at the private parts of anyone during his or her training for that profession, unless he would be repelling serious harm from a Muslim in the process—even if in future— depends upon that.

351. It is not obligatory for a Muslim to investigate to ensure that the medicine [given to him] does not consist of forbidden ingredients, even if that inquiring and ensuring is easy for him.

Question and Answers

352. **Question:** The serious harm of narcotic drugs to the user or society in general (whether from being addicted to it or other [societal, familial, and ethical] perspectives) is well known. Therefore, the doctors and health care professionals are strongly opposing it and the laws governing the society also strongly combat it. So what is the view of the noble *shari'a* on this matter?

Answer: By considering the serious harm of narcotic drugs, it is forbidden to use them due to the great damage they cause. Based on obligatory precaution, it is compulsory to refrain from using them any way [even if there is no harm], except for medical purposes and the like; in the latter case, it can be used only to the extent of need. And Allãh knows the best.

353. Question: Medical literature states that **smoking** is the main cause for heart and cancer diseases, and it also shortens the life span of the smoker. So what is the rule on smoking concerning (a) the beginner, (b) the addicted, (c) the passive smoker? In the third case, the medical experts say that the smoke also harms a person sitting besides a smoker; so what would be the rule if he considers the passive smoking to be of considerable harm?

Answer: (a) Smoking becomes harãm for the beginner if it entails serious harm, even in future regardless of whether that serious harm is certain or most probable or just probable to the level that sensible people would demand caution. However, with the protection from serious harm (for example, by smoking less frequently), there is no problem in it.

(b) If continuing to smoke will cause serious harm to the addict —as explained above— it is necessary for him to refrain from it unless the harm in quitting is similar or greater to the harm in continuing, or the great difficulty that he will face in quitting is such that it cannot be normally tolerated.

(c) The same rule as explained in (a) for the beginner, applies in this case also.

354. Question: Some people believe that a brain-dead person is a dead person, even if the heart has not yet stopped and that it will definitely stop after that. This is what the doctors say. Is a person who has been pronounced brain-dead be considered as dead even if his heart is still working?

Answer: The criterion in applying the term "dead" in so far as the application of religious laws goes is the common perception of people, in the sense that they would call him "dead". And this is not proven in the situation mentioned in the question.

355. Question: The medical profession demands that the doctor check his female patients carefully; and since getting undressed for medical check up is common in some European countries, is it permissible to engage in medical practice here under such circumstances?

Answer: It is permissible if one refrains from looking and touching in the harãm way, except to the extent where the check up of the patient requires.

356. Question: Sometimes the practising physician feels that he has to uncover certain parts, other than the private parts, of the female patient [for examination]. Is it permissible for him to uncover her body in the following circumstances:

(One) When a female physician is available but it will be very expensive?

(Two) When the patient is not in danger, although she is sick regardless?

(Three) What is the rule if the part that the physician has to examine is a private part?

Answer: (a) If visiting a female physician is possible, it is not permissible [for a female patient to uncover her body for a male physician] unless the cost is so much that it will hurt her financial situation.

(b) It is permissible if not visiting that male physician will harm [her health-wise] or put her in a serious inconvenience that is not normally tolerated.

(c) The rule is the same as explained above; and in both the cases, he must uncover only the parts that need examining. And if it is possible to treat the case without looking directly at the parts that are harãm to be looked at (for example, if he can see through a monitor or a mirror), that should be the course of action, based on precaution.

357. Question: Some experts of genetic engineering claim that they can improve the human race by altering the genes in the following ways:

(a) Removing the ugliness of the face;

(b) Replacing it with beautiful characteristics;

(c) By both of the above.

Is it permissible for the scientists to engage in these kinds of activities? Is it permissible for a Muslim to allow the doctors to alter his genes?

Answer: If there are no side effects, then, in principle, there is no problem in it.

358. Question: Pharmaceutical companies in the West run tests on their drugs before selling them in the market. Is it permissible for a doctor to use a drug on his patient —without the knowledge of the patient— before its testing period is over thinking that that particular drug would cure the disease?

Answer: It is necessary to inform the patient about the situation and seek his consent on using the drug on him except when he is sure that the drug would not cause side effects and that the doubt is only about its benefit.

359. Question: In certain cases, some governmental agencies demand that autopsy be performed on the body of the deceased to establish the cause of death. When is it permissible to agree to their demand and when is it not?

Answer: No heir of a deceased Muslim is allowed to give consent for autopsy of the deceased for the purpose mentioned above and other similar purposes; and it is necessary for him to prevent the autopsy if possible. Of course, if another important factor is involved that is equal or more important than this basic rule, it is permissible.

360. Question: Is donating an organ from a living person to another living person (for example, in case of a kidney) or from a dead person by his will to a living person permissible? Would the ruling be different if it were from a Muslim to a non-Muslim or vice versa? Is the rule for certain organs different from other organs?

Answer: As far as donating an organ from a living person to the body of another person is concerned, there is no problem in it if it does not entail a serious harm to the donar. (For example, donating one kidney by a person who has another healthy kidney.)

As far as removing an organ from a deceased (based on his will) for the purpose of transplanting it into a living person is concerned, there is no problem in it as long as:

(a) The deceased was not a Muslim or someone who is considered a Muslim.

(b) Or the life of a Muslim depended on such transplantation.

In other than these two cases, there is a problem in enforcing the will [of the deceased] and in allowing the removal of the organ. However, if the will had been done [by the deceased], there will be no indemnity on the person retrieving the organ from the dead body.

361. Question: If an organ of an atheist is transplanted in a Muslim's body, would it be considered ritually pure *(tāhir)* when it is considered, after transplantation, as part of the Muslim's body?

Answer: An organ extracted from the body is ritually impure *(najis)* irrespective of whether it came from a Muslim or a non-Muslim. And when it becomes, by the rejuvenation, part of a Muslim's body or of someone who is to be considered a Muslim, it becomes *tāhir*.

362. Question: Insulin used for treatment of diabetics is sometimes extracted from the pancreas of pigs. Can we use it?

Answer: There is no problem in injecting insulin in the muscles, veins or under the skin.

363. **Question:** Is it permissible to transplant the liver of pig in a human body?

Answer: It is permissible to transplant pig's liver into the body of a human being. And Allāh knows the best.

364. **Question:** Is the process of test-tube babies allowed? In the sense that the wife's ovum and the husband's sperm are extracted to be fertilized outside the body, and then placed in the womb [of the wife].

Answer: In principle, it is allowed.

365. **Question:** There are certain hereditary diseases that are transferred from parents to children and pose a danger to their lives in the future. Modern science has acquired the means of preventing some of such diseases by fertilizing the woman's ovum in a test tube, and then examining the genes and eliminating the problematic ones. Then it is again placed into the woman's womb. The remaining genes [i.e., ova] are destroyed. Is this religiously permissible?

Answer: In principle, there is no problem in it.

366. **Question:** In the process of fertilization in a lab, more than one ovum is fertilized at a time. Knowing that implanting all fertilized ova in the mother's womb will endanger her life. Is it permissible for us to use only one fertilized ovum and destroy the remaining ones?

Answer: It is not obligatory to implant all the ova fertilized by sperm in a test tube into the womb. Therefore, it is permissible to use one ovum and destroy the remaining ones.

367. **Question:** Is it permissible to engage in embellishing the face and the body [of another person]?

Answer: It is permissible provided one refrains from looking and touching what is harãm to be looked at or touched.

AIDS

AIDS or Acquired Immune Deficiency Syndrome is a disease that has afflicted, based on 1996 data, eight million people worldwide and there are about twenty-two million who carry the AIDS virus. The latest data show that one and a half million people have died of AIDS in the year 1996 only bringing the total number of those who died of that disease to six million! This was announced by World Health Organization on the International Aids Day on 1 December 1996.

Doctors have identified the following ways in which AIDS is inflicted:

(One) Sexual intercourse between members of the same sex or the opposite sex [in which one member is already afflicted]. This represents the most dangerous and widespread method of the spread of AIDS. The chance of infliction through this method is 80%.

(Two) Through blood vessels: by transfusion; by injection (especially in the case of drug addicts); by open wounds; and organ transplantation, and even through surgery if the instruments are not properly sanitized.

(Three) The feotus can be afflicted while in the womb or at the time of birth if the mother is already afflicted with AIDS.

The data indicate that this disease has affected all countries and that no nation is immune from it; and that the majority of the afflicted people are males. Diseases that had been eradicated have again started spreading because of the AIDS problem (e.g., pulmonary tuberculosis).

In this background, we presented the following questions to his eminence, Ayatullah Sistani:

368. **Question:** What is the rule concerning isolating a person afflicted with AIDS? Is it obligatory upon him to isolate himself? Is it obligatory on his family to isolate him [from the public]?

Answer: It is not obligatory upon him to isolate himself just as it is not obligatory upon others to do so. Indeed, it wouldn't be permissible to prevent him from frequenting public places like masjid, etc, as long as there is no danger of infecting the others with the virus. It is, however, obligatory for him as well as others to be careful in situations where there exists certainty or probability of infecting others.

369. Question: What is the rule on intentionally infecting others with the AIDS virus?

Answer: This is not allowed. If it leads —even after passage of some time— to the death of the person who has been infected, then the heirs of the deceased have the right of retribution against the person responsible for infecting, provided the latter was aware that that infection could lead to death; but if he was ignorant of that effect or unaware of it at that time, only indemnity (blood money) and penalty would apply.

370. Question: Is it permissible for a person infected with AIDS to marry a person who is free from it?

Answer: Yes; but it is not permissible for him or her to mislead by deliberately presenting himself or herself as free from AIDS at the time of proposing while they are not. Similarly, it is not permissible for him or her to become intimate in a way that would infect the other spouse.

However, if there is only a probability of infection and no certainty, then it is not obligatory for him or her to refrain from intimacy provided there is agreement on it.

371. Question: What is the ruling on marriage between two people who are carriers of the AIDS virus?

Answer: There is no problem in it. However, if sexual relation between them will intensify the disease to a serious level, it is necessary for them to refrain from it.

372. Question: What is the ruling on sexual relations for a person who is infected with AIDS? Is it permissible for a non-infected person to refuse sexual relation with their spouse because sexual intercourse is one of the main methods of spreading the virus?

Answer: It is permissible for a non-infected wife not to make herself available to her infected husband for intimacy that could lead to infection by the virus. It is indeed obligatory upon her to prevent him from such intimacy.

If it is possible to lessen the chances of infection to a level that is insignificant —for example, 2%— by using condom, etc, it is permissible for her to be intimate to her husband. In such a case, it would, based on precaution, not be permissible for her to refuse [intimate relations with her husband].

This clarifies also the case of a non-afflicted husband and an afflicted wife: it is not permissible for him to have sexual relations with her with what sensible people perceive as considerable risk— of being infected by the virus. In such a case, the right of wife to have sexual relations [at least once] every four months is suspended except when it becomes possible to adopt methods that would properly prevent infection with the virus.

373. Question: What is the ruling concerning the right of the non-infected spouse in seeking separation?

Answer: If deception was involved in the marriage in the sense that the husband or the wife concealed the fact that they have AIDS at the time of proposing, engagement, and the marriage contract *('aqd)* was recited based on that understanding — the deceived party has the right of annulment.

However, if the wife or her representative was silent about the issue of the disease and the husband assumed that she is free from it, the silence does not count as deception and, therefore, it does not yield the right of annulment.

If there was no deception or the disease flared up after the marriage, the non-infected husband has the right to divorcing his infected wife.

Does the non-infected wife have the right to ask for divorce from her infected husband on the grounds that she is being deprived of her conjugal rights?

There are two views [on this]; precaution should not be ruled out in this case. Of course, if her husband abandons her completely and she becomes like a suspended woman [neither married nor unmarried], it is permissible for her to take her case to the religious judge[117] to force her husband to choose one of two courses: either end the abandonment or divorce her.

374. Question: What is the ruling on the divorce of a woman whose husband is infected with AIDS?

Answer: It has already been mentioned above.

375. Question: What is the ruling on abortion for a pregnant woman who is infected with AIDS?

Answer: It is not permissible, more so after the soul has entered the feotus. Of course, if continuation of the pregnancy constitutes a danger to the mother, it is permissible for her to abort it before the entering of the soul in the feotus, but not after it.

376. Question: What is ruling on the custody of an infected mother with regard to her non-infected baby and also on breast-feeding?

Answer: She does not lose the right of custody of her baby; but she must adopt sufficient methods to ensure that the virus does not infect the baby. If it is probable —a considerable probability— that the virus may be transmitted

---

[117] Translator's Note: "Religious judge" means the mujtahid or someone authorized by him in judicial matters.

through breast-feeding, it is necessary for her to refrain from it.

377. Question: What is the ruling on considering AIDS as terminal illness?

Answer: Since this disease lasts long, what can be classified as terminal is its last stage only which is closer to death brought about by the disruption and complete destruction of the immune system or the occurrence of fatal nervous breakdown.

378. Question: When a person is diagnosed as having ADIS, is it permissible for the doctor or is it obligatory upon him to inform the patient's like relatives, especially their spouse?

Answer: It is permissible to inform them, if the patient or his guardian gives consent. It is obligatory if the survival —for a longer time span— of the patient depends on it. It is similarly obligatory if he knows that by not informing them, the virus would infect them for not taking necessary precautions. And Allāh knows the best.

379. Question: If a Muslim knows that contracted AIDS, is it permissible for him to engage in sexual relations with his wife? Is it obligatory for him to inform his wife about it?

Answer: If he knows that the virus can infect her through sexual relations, it is not permissible for him at all. Similarly [it is obligatory on him to refrain from sex] if there exists a considerable level of likelihood [of infection] except in the case where the wife knows about it and agrees to it.

* * *

```
┌─────────────────────────────────────────┐
│                                           │
│           Chapter Seven                   │
│                                           │
│           MARRIAGE                        │
│                                           │
└─────────────────────────────────────────┘
```

Introduction

The Islamic legal system regulates the relationship between members of the opposite sex covering its various important aspects and expanding on its details since it is an important need of the human race and many issues related to the individual and the society are based on it.

There are many rules concerning the relationship between man and woman, but here I shall confine myself to only to the ones that are relevant to Muslims residing in non-Muslim countries.

General Rules

380. Marriage is among highly recommended deeds. The Prophet has said, "Whosoever marries, he has protected half of his religion."[118] He also said, "Whoever likes to follow my

---

[118] *Wasā'ilu 'sh-Shī'a,* vol. 20, p. 17.

202 ■ *A Code of Practice for Muslims in the West*

tradition, then [he should know that] marriage is of my tradition."[119] Again he said, "No Muslim man has gained a benefit besides Islam better than a Muslim wife who is a cause of his pleasure whenever he looks at her, who obeys him when he commands her, and remains faithful to him when he is away."[120]

381. Man should give importance to the qualities of the woman he would like to marry. He should not marry except a woman who is chaste, honourable, of good lineage, and righteous who will help him in the affairs of this world and the hereafter.

Man should not confine his choice to her physical beauty and wealth. It has been narrated from the Prophet (s.a.w.) that he said, "O People! Beware of the green grass [growing] in a waste site." Someone asked, "O Messenger of Allāh! And what is the green grass in a waste site?" He replied, "A beautiful woman in an evil environment."[121]

382. The woman and her guardians should give importance to the qualities of the man she chooses to marry. She should not marry except a man who is religious, chaste, of good character, not a drunkard or someone who commits sins and evil deeds.

383. It is better not to reject the proposition of a man who is religious and of good character. The Prophet has said, "When a man whose religion and character pleases you comes to you [with a proposition], then marry him. If you do not do so, there will be chaos and a great corruption in the world."[122]

---

[119]   Ibid, p. 18.
[120]   As-Sistāni, *Minhāju 's-Sāliheen,* vol. 2, p. 7.
[121]   *Wasā'ilu 'sh-Shí'a,* vol. 20, p. 35.
[122]   At-Tusi, *Tahdhíbu 'l-Ahkām,* vol. 7, p. 395. Also see the chapter on compitability in marriage in the same book, p. 394ff.

384. It is mustahab (recommended) to work in getting people married, in being intermediary, and in bringing the two parties to an agreement.

385. It is permissible for a man to look at the attractive features of the woman he intends to marry. Similarly, it is permissible to talk to her before proposing. So, it is permissible to look at her face, hair, neck, hands and wrists, and legs and other parts of her body, provided that he does not do so with sexually lustful intention. (See the question-answer section below.)

386. In Islamic law, marriage is of two kinds: permanent and temporary.

Permanent Marriage means the marriage in which there is no fixed time limit. The wife in this marriage is known as "the permanent wife".[123]

Temporary Marriage means the marriage in which the time limit is fixed to a year or more or less. The wife in this marriage is known as "the temporary wife".[124]

387. The formula for solemnizing the permanent marriage is as follows: The woman says to the man: "*Zawwaj-tuka nafsi bi mahrin qadruhu* x — I give myself to you in marriage for the marriage gift which is x." (In place of "x" mention the agreed upon marriage dowry [*mahr*].) The man immediately says, "*Qabiltut tazweej* — I accept the marriage."

The formula for solemnizing the temporary marriage is as follows: The woman says to the man: ""*Zawwaj-tuka nafsi bi mahrin qadruhu* (x) *li muddati* (x) — I give myself to you in marriage for the dowry of (x) for the time period (x)." (In

---

[123] For more information on marriage and its laws, see Sayyid 'Izzu 'd-Dín Bahru 'l-'Ulûm, *az-Ziwāj fi 'l-Qur'ān wa 's-Sunnah.* [Also see Sayyid Muhammad Rizvi, *Marriage and Morals in Islam.*]

[124] For more information on temporary marriage and its laws, see Sayyid Muhammad Taqi al-Hakím, *az-Ziwāju 'l-Muwaqqat wa Dawruhu fi Halli Mushkilāti 'l-Jins.*

place of first "x" mention the agreed upon *mahr* and in place of the second "x" mention the agreed upon time.) The man immediately says, *"Qabiltut tazweej* — I accept the marriage."

388. It is permissible for the couple to recite the formula of marriage agreement by themselves or by appointing a representative who will recite it on their behalf. There is no condition for the presence of witnesses during the solemnization of the marriage, just as the presence of a religious scholar is not a condition for the validity of the marriage.

389. For a person who cannot recite the formula of marriage in Arabic, it is permissible to say it in a language that would convey the meaning of marriage even when he can appoint someone to say it in Arabic.

390. A Muslim man is allowed to marry a Christian or a Jewish woman in temporary marriage. Based on precaution, it is obligatory to refrain from marrying a non-Muslim woman in permanent marriage.

A Muslim man is not allowed to marry a non-Muslim woman from other than Ahlul Kitab, neither permanently nor temporarily. Based on obligatory precaution, a Muslim man must refrain from marrying a Zoroastrian woman even temporarily.

As for a Muslim woman, she is not allowed to marry a non-Muslim man at all. (See the question-answer section below.)

391. In marrying a virgin girl, whether Muslim or from Ahlul Kitab, it is necessary to get the consent of her father or paternal grandfather if she is not independent in the affairs of her life.

However, it is precautionarily obligatory to seek their consent [i.e., of the father or the paternal grandfather] even if she is independent in her affairs.

Consent of her brother, mother, sister or other relations is not required.

392. The consent of the father or the paternal grandfather to marry a virgin girl, who is both adult and sensible, is not required [in the following cases:]

[a] if they stop her from marrying someone who is her equal both according to shar'ia and common practice;

[b] if they completely withdraw from involvement in her marriage;

[c] when it is not possible to get their consent because of their absence.

In these cases, she is permitted to marry if she is in need of marriage.

393. The consent of the father or the paternal grandfather is not required in marriage of a non-virgin woman (that is, a girl who had previously married and had sexual intercourse). But the case of the woman who had lost her virginity because of fornication or another cause is like that of a virgin.

394. In countries where the majority consists of atheists and Ahlul Kitab, i.e. non-Muslims, it is necessary for a Muslim to ask the woman whom he wants to marry about her religion so that he may ensure that she is not an atheist and so that his marriage be valid. Her answer [about her faith and religion] is to be accepted.

395. A Muslim man who is married to a Muslim woman is not allowed, in his concurrent second marriage, to marry an Ahlul Kitab woman, (a Jew or a Christian), without asking consent of his Muslim wife.

Based on obligatory precaution, he should refrain from marrying her, even in the temporary form and even if his Muslim wife consents to that. The presence of the Muslim wife with him or otherwise is immaterial. (See the question-answer section below.)

396. It is not permissible to engage in sexual relations with an Ahlul Kitab woman without marriage contract, even if the government of her country is in the state of war with Muslims. (See the question-answer section below.)

397. Based on obligatory precaution, one should refrain from marrying a woman famous for adultery unless she repents. Similarly, based on obligatory precaution, the adulterer should not marry the woman with whom he committed adultery unless after she repents. (See the question-answer section below.)

398. If the marriages that took place among non-Muslims is valid according to their custom, such marriage is also considered valid by us irrespective of whether the spouses are both Ahlul Kitab, both non-Ahlul Kitab, or one is an Ahlul Kitab and the other is non-Ahlul Kitab. When both spouses embrace Islam together, they will stay married based on the past marriage, i.e. there would be no need to recite the marriage formula anew according to the tradition of our religion and school of thought.

399. If the father withdraws his guardianship from his virgin daughter and considers her independent. After reaching the age of eighteen as is common in the West, it is permissible to marry her without getting the consent and approval of her father.

400. "It is permissible for the husband and wife to look at the body of one another, outside and inside, including the private parts; and also to touch any part of one another with any part of their own body with lust and without it."[125]

401. It is obligatory on the husband to provide for the wife if she is a permanent wife and obedient to him in matters in which she is required to obey him. In this case, it is obligatory

---

[125]   Ibid, p. 11.

on the husband to provide whatever the wife needs in her life like food, dress, and accommodation with the required amenities like fan, air-conditioner, carpets, furniture, etc. that are commensurate with her status as his wife. Such status would differ according to place, time, circumstances, common perceptions, customs, standard of living, etc. (See the question-answer section below.)

402. It is obligatory on the husband to pay for his wife when he asks her to accompany him in his travels. It is similarly obligatory for him to provide travelling expenses when she goes on a journey that is necessarily connected to the affairs of her life. For example, if she is sick and her treatment depends on traveling to a specialist, it is obligatory on the husband to pay for the expenses, her ticket as well as medical charges.

403. "It is not permissible to neglect sexual relations with a young wife for more than four months unless there is an excuse like unbearable difficulty or harm [in fulfillment of that duty] or unless she agrees to it [that is, forgoes her conjugal rights] or if it was part of their agreement at the time of marriage.

"Based on obligatory precaution, this rule is not limited to the permanent wife, i.e. it includes the temporary wife also. Similarly, based on obligatory precaution, it is not restricted to the husband who is present, it also includes the husband who is travelling. Therefore, it would not be permissible for him to prolong his journey, (without valid reason), if it entails depriving the wife of her right, more so when the journey is not viewed as essential in people's eyes, like a vacation and entertainment."[126]

---

[126] As-Sayyid as-Sistāni, *Minhāju 's-Sāliheen,* vol. 2, p. 10-11; also see the last reference.

404. "It is not permissible for a Muslim woman to marry a non-Muslim man in permanent or temporary marriage."[127]

405. "If the husband harasses his wife and is spiteful towards her without any valid reason, it is permissible for her to present her case to the religious judge who will force him to live with her in an amicable manner if that is possible, or censure him as he seems fit. If that also does not work, she can demand divorce from the husband. If he refuses to divorce her and it is not possible to force him to divorce her, the religious judge will pronounce her divorced."[128] (See the question-answer section below.)

406. It is permissible to artificially inseminate the wife with her husband's sperm, provided that the process of insemination does not involve a harām act like looking at parts that are forbidden for a person and other harām acts. (See the question-answer section below.)

407. It is permissible for a woman to use contraceptives (the pill) to prevent pregnancy provided it does not damage her health in a serious manner, irrespective of whether or not the husband has agreed to it.

408. It is permissible for a woman to use Intrauterine Devices (IUD) and other methods that prevent pregnancy provided they do not entail serious harm to the woman's health and provided that the insertion of the device does not involve a harām act like the male touching or looking at the parts of the woman's body that are forbidden for him to look at. Similarly, it should not involve the female looking at and touching without gloves the private parts because that are harām to touch or look at. Moreover, the IUD should not cause the

---

[127] Ibid, p. 67.
[128] As-Sayyid as-Sistāni, *Minhāju 's-Sāliheen,* vol. 2, p. 109.

abortion of the fertilized ovum after its implantation [in the womb].[129]

409. It is not permissible for a woman to abort the feotus after the soul has entered into it, irrespective of the reason for abortion.

It is permissible to abort the feotus before the soul enters it if there is an unbearable harm to the mother in continuing the pregnancy or it becomes extremely difficult for her. (See the question-answer section below.)

410. If the mother aborts the feotus by herself, she is liable for the indemnity. Similarly, if the father or a third person like a doctor caused the abortion, the indemnity is payable by that person. (See the question-answer section below.)

There are other details and rules regarding the issue of abortion in the Manuals of Islamic Laws and other books of Islamic jurisprudence.[130]

Questions and Answers

411. Question: Is it permissible for us to give Imam's portion of *khums* for the marriage of a believer (mo'min) in the West knowing that the amount of money that is given here [for this one marriage] can be used for marriages of more than one believer [in the Muslim countries], and there are many needy believer, in Muslim countries? Is it not necessary that most possible number of deserving people should be helped from *sahm-e* Imam?

---

[129] Translator's Note: "The medical experts do not exactly know how IUD works. Presently there are two opinions: one says that the IUD prevents fertilization; and the other says that it prevents the fertilized ovum from implantation onto the uterus. Since the shar'í pregnancy begins at implantation, there is no problem in using the IUD as a birth control device irrespective of the above differences among professionals." *Marriage & Morals in Islam* (Toronto: IEIC, Revised Edition, 1994) p. 121.

[130] See as-Sistāni, *Minhāju 's-Sāliheen,* vol. 2, p. 136-137 as well as his *al-Masā'ilu 'l-Muntakhaba,* p. 385-419.

Answer: Although providing for the marriage of needy believers is among the uses of the portion of the Imam (a.s.), one is not permitted to utilize it for this or its other purposes without the permission of the *marja'* or his representative.

It is not necessary to use the *sahm-e* Imam among the most possible number of deserving people; what is important is to prioritize the important causes. This prioritization varies according to circumstances.

412. Question: Is it sufficient for a non-Arab to pronounce the marriage formula in Arabic without understanding the meaning of the words, even though we know that the purpose for uttering those words is to solemnize the marriage in the right way?

And is it necessary to say it in Arabic, supposing that just the utterance is sufficient, without having the need to say the marriage formula in another language?

Answer: It would be sufficient, provided that the person has some understanding, even roughly, of the meaning of the words [in Arabic]; based on obligatory precaution, it would not be sufficient to pronounce it in another language.

413. Question: Is it valid to pronounce the marriage formula through a telephone?

Answer: It is valid.

414. Question: Is it possible to bear witness using the telephone or fax or mail letter?

Answer: The rules and consequences that apply to the bearing of witness in presence of a judge cannot materialize without the physical presence of the witness. As for the testimony that just deals with describing the incident the way it occurred, the methods mentioned above and other methods similar to them are sufficient, provided that they are secured from compulsion and error.

415. Question: Is it permissible to look carefully at the body, with exception of private parts, of the woman one intends to marry with lust or without lust?

Answer: It is permissible to look at her features like the face, the hair, and the hands but without lustful intention. And [it is permissible] even if one knows that lustful thoughts will naturally occur [by looking at her].

When a person has come to know about her features by the first look, it is not permissible to look again.

416. Question: Some Western governments allow the daughter to be independent of her parents, both, financially and physically, after she has passed the age of sixteen. If she seeks her parents advice, it is only for seeking their opinion or out of respect for them. Is such a virgin girl allowed to marry, in a permanent or a temporary form, without the consent of her father?

Answer: If this means that the father has allowed her to marry whomsoever she wants or that he has withdrawn from interfering in the matter of her marriage, it is permissible for her to do so; otherwise, based on obligatory precaution, it is not permissible.

417. Question: If a woman is over thirty years of age and is still virgin, is it necessary for her to seek the permission of her guardian for marriage?

Answer: If she is not independent in her own affairs, it is obligatory on her to seek his consent; rather even if she is independent, she must seek his consent, as a matter of compulsory precaution.

418. Question: Is it permissible for a virgin girl to use the light beauty powder in order to draw attention [to herself] in gatherings that are exclusively for ladies? What if she does so with the purpose of seeking marriage — wouldn't it be counted as concealing physical defects, [if there were any]?

Answer: It is permissible for her to do that and it would not be counted as "concealing the physical defects". Even if it were counted as such, it would not be harām unless she was intent on deceiving the person who wants to marry her.

419. Question: When is it permissible for a wife to ask for divorce through the religious judge? Is it permissible for a wife — whose husband constantly treats her badly or a wife whose is sexually not satisfied by her husband to an extent that she fears committing that which is *harām* — to ask for divorce and be divorced?

Answer: It is permissible for her to ask for divorce through the religious judge if her husband refuses to fulfill her marital rights and also refuses to divorce her after the religious judge has ordered him to do one of the two. In such a case, the judge would pronounce the divorce for the wife.

The circumstances in which this could happen are the followings:

(a) When the husband refuses to provide for the wife and also refuses to divorce her. This would include the case of a husband who is unable to provide for his wife and also refuses to divorce her.

(b) When the husband harasses the wife, treats her unjustly, and does not behave with her kindly as Almighty Allāh has ordered him to do.

(c) When the husband abandons her completely and she becomes like a suspended woman neither married nor free to marry.

As for the case where he does not fully satisfy her sexual needs to an extent that she fears committing the *harām,* then, based on compulsory precaution, the husband must fulfill her needs or consent to her demand for divorce. However, if he does not do that, then the wife has to bear the situation patiently and wait [for a better future].

420. **Question:** There is a Muslim woman whose husband has left her for a long time now so much so that there is no hope of her getting together with her husband in the near future; she claims that she cannot stay without a husband because of the difficulty in living as a single woman in the West where she fears robbery and stealing by break-ins into the house. Can she ask for divorce through the religious judge so that he may pronounce the divorce and she can then marry whosoever she wants?

Answer: If the husband has abandoned her, she can take her case to the religious judge who will then force the husband to choose one of two courses: either end the abandonment or release her [by divorce] so that she can marry someone else. If he refuses to do any of the two and it is not possible to force him to adopt one of the two alternatives, the religious judge has the right to pronounce the divorce on her request.

But if the wife is the one who has left her husband without any [valid] justification, there is no way for the religious judge to pronounce her divorce.

421. **Question:** A Muslim couple got separated for a long time. Is it permissible for him to marry, temporarily or permanently, a woman from Ahlul Kitab without the knowledge of his Muslim wife? Is it permissible for him to marry if he asks his Muslim wife for her consent to his marriage and she agrees to it?

Answer: For a Muslim man to marry a woman from Ahlul Kitab permanently is against the compulsory precaution under any circumstance.

And his marriage to a Jewish and a Christian woman on a temporary basis is allowed, only if he is not already married to a Muslim wife. If he has a Muslim wife, temporary marriage with an Ahlul Kitab woman is not permissible without her consent; nay, even with her consent it is not permissible, based on compulsory precaution.

422. Question: A Muslim man who is married to a Muslim woman migrated for years from his country. Now he wants to embark on temporary marriage with a woman from Ahlul Kitab just a few days after divorcing his Muslim wife. Is this permissible for him while his Muslim wife is still in her waiting period *(al-'idda)*?

Answer: The temporary marriage mentioned in the question is considered invalid because the wife who is in the waiting period of the revocable divorce is still considered as a wife. And it has just been mentioned that to marry an Ahlul Kitab woman in temporary marriage while one has a Muslim wife is not permissible [as a matter of compulsary precaution].

423. Question: Is it obligatory to inform the man who wants to marry a woman from the Ahlul Kitab or a Muslim woman that she has not yet observed the waiting period *('idda)* from the divorce of her past husband, or that she is still in the *'idda* [during which marriage is forbidden for her]?

Answer: It is not obligatory.

424. Question: Is it permissible for a Muslim man to marry a non-Muslim woman who is still married to a non-Muslim man? Is there an *'idda* period for her when she separates from her non-Muslim husband? What is the period of that *'idda?* Is it permissible to have sexual relations with her during the time when she is in the *'idda* from her non-Muslim husband? If she embraces Islam, how long will be her *'idda* from her non-Muslim husband if she intends to marry a Muslim man?

Answer: It is not permissible to marry her while she is married to a non-Muslim in a marriage which is recognized by them because she is a married woman. It is permissible to marry her temporarily after her divorce and after the completion of the '*idda* from her non-Muslim husband. (The period of her '*idda* is not different from the '*idda* of a Muslim woman.) Therefore, it is not permissible before the completion of the '*idda*.

If she becomes a Muslim after having had sexual relations with her non-Muslim husband and the husband has not embraced Islam, it is precuationarily obligatory for a Muslim not to marry her until after the completion of her '*idda*. But if she became a Muslim without having ever established sexual relations with her non-Muslim husband, then their marriage will be annulled immediately and there is no '*idda* in such a case.

425. Question: What is the meaning of "justice" required by religious law in dealing with one's wives?

Answer: The justice that is required [in dealing with polygamy] is related to the division [of time between them] in the sense that when he spends a night with one of them then, he must spend one night each with the rest of them in every four nights.

The justice that is required as a recommendation is equality in spending money, giving attention, cheerfulness, and fulfillment of their sexual desire, etc.

426. Question: If a Muslim woman commits adultery, is it permissible for her husband to kill her?

Answer: Based on obligatory precaution, it is not permissible for him to kill her, even if he sees her in the act of committing adultery.

427. Question: What is meant by the expression "an adulterous woman known for adultery" that is used in the Manuals of Islamic Laws?

Answer: It means that such a woman is known among the people for committing adultery.

428. Question: Is it permissible to be party to temporary marriage with a woman who is "known for adultery" if no other woman is available and the youth is in desperate need of marriage?

Answer: Based on obligatory precaution, one should refrain from marrying such a woman except after her repentance.

429. Question: What is the meaning of the expression used by the jurists that "there is no waiting period (*'idda*) for an adulterous woman because of her adultery"?

Answer: It means that she is allowed to marry after having committed adultery without observing the *'idda;* and, if she is married, then it is permissible for her husband to have sexual relations with her without observing the *'idda* except in the case of *al-wat'i bis-shubha* (sexual relation established based on mistaken identity or ignorance of the law).

430. Question: A man lived with a woman whom he intended to marry and also had sex with her without entering into marriage contract (*'aqd*); thereafter he married her in the proper religious way. Is her co-habitation before the *'aqd* considered marriage in the eyes of religious law? Does the subsequent *'aqd* have retroactive effect? What will be the status of the children born before the *'aqd?*

Answer: In [an Islamic] marriage, the spousal relationship is established by the verbal expression of the proposal and the acceptance, and no action or deed that reflects the intention of marriage can be a substitute for the spoken words. Consequently, the marriage mentioned in the question is not valid except after the pronouncement of the religious marriage formula that does not have any retroactive effect.

As for the children, they will be considered legitimate if the parents did not know the law [requiring the *'aqd*] because then their relationship will be classified as *"wat'i bis-shubha"*. But if both were aware of the law, their relationship is considered as adultery and consequently the children will be illegitimate. However, if only one knew about the law without the other, the child will be a legitimate child in relation to the ignorant parent only.

431. Question: Certain circumstances demand that the use of insemination between husband and wife in order to increase the chances of pregnancy; this process of insemination requires exposing the private parts for the doctor. Is this allowed?

Answer: Exposing the private parts for the purpose mentioned above is not allowed. However, if there is a need that compels one to have children, and having children requires exposing the private parts, it is allowed. An example of "need" is when enduring childlessness becomes an unbearable difficulty for the couple.

432. Question: A woman who does not want children asks the doctor to tie her falopian tubes. Is this permissible for her—no matter whether it is reversible or irreversible; and whether or not the husband agrees to it?

Answer: It is permissible for her provided that it does not involve any *harām* touching or looking, irrespective of whether or not it is reversible. The permission of the husband is not required; of course, his permission might be required for other considerations.

433. Question: In the West [more precisely, in Italy] an ovum of a woman was fertilized in the laboratory, then the fertilized ovum was implanted in the womb of the mother; the feotus developed in and was born from the grandmother's womb. Is it permissible to implant a feotus [or the fertilized ovum] in its grandmother's womb? And who will be the child's mother according to the *shariʿa*?

Answer: It is difficult to consider it permissible in principle, even if we overlook the *harām* looking and touching that is involved in this kind of procedure. And if this process takes place and the child is born, then in determining who is to be considered the child's mother from the genealogical perspective —the genetic mother or the biological mother— there are two views. It is prudent to observe caution in regard to both women. [That is, fulfill the rights of mother in regard to both.]

434. Question: Sometimes the sperm of a man is preserved in a sperm bank. Is it permissible for a divorced Muslim woman to use the sperm of a strange man [to artificially inseminate herself] with or without his permission and without recitation of marriage formula? What is the ruling if the sperm is that of her ex-husband, and she intends to use it during the waiting period or after that period?

Answer: It is not permissible for a woman to inseminate herself with the sperm of a strange man; and it is permissible to do so with the sperm of her husband even during the waiting period but not after that.

435. Question: A man is put in a situation that he either pleases his family or pleases his wife: should he divorce his wife in order to please his family or should he do the opposite?

Answer: He should adopt the situation that is best for his religion as well as his world, that he should be inclined towards justice and equitability, and refrain from injustice and violation of the rights [of others].

436. Question: What is the meaning of "obligatory maintenance" that a husband must provide for his wife? Should the level of the support be according to the social standing of the husband or according to the standard of life that the wife was used to in her father's home or other than that?

Answer: The criterion is the level that would be appropriate for her status in relation to that of her husband.

[That is, the level that would be appropriate for her "as the wife of her husband".]

437. Question: The wife has certain rights upon the husband; now if the husband neglects some of those rights, is it permissible for the wife to ignore his sexual advances?

Answer: She does not have that; if counseling and then warning do not help [in changing the husband's attitude], she can take her problem to the religious judge who should take appropriate action.

438. Question: On embarking on a journey or coming back, a Muslim traveller embraces and kisses his wife in public. Is this permissible for him?

Answer: It is not harãm to do that if the rules of appropriate covering [of the clothes] and *hijãb* are observed and as long as it does not entice lust [in other people]; it is preferable to refrain from this kind of behaviour.

439. Question: Legal divorce according to Western laws had already taken place between a man and his wife. The husband is not willing to uphold her religious rights, neither does he pay any maintenance money for her and refuses to listen to the religious authorities who work as go-betweens. What should the wife do knowing well that her patience under such circumstances will surely cause her [unbearable] difficulty?

Answer: She should present her problem to the religious judge or his authorized representative who will then convey to the husband to either provide for her or grant her religious divorce—even by appointing someone else to do that. If he refuses to do either, and it is not possible [for the religious judge] to provide for her from the husband's wealth, the judge or his representative will pronounce the divorce for her.

440. Question: Is it permissible to have sex with a non-Muslim woman —from Ahlul Kitab or atheist— without doing the religious marriage on the basis that her country is in state of war, directly or indirectly, against the Muslims?

Answer: This is not allowed.

441. Question: A wife neither obeys her husband nor fulfills her marital duties; she also goes out without his permission to stay with her own family for seven months. Then instead of having recourse to Islamic laws, she goes to a non-Islamic court in order to get spousal maintenance, custody of the children, and divorce from her husband. Does such a wife have a right in getting anything from her husband? In such a situation, when she goes to non-Islamic court it will apply non-Islamic laws to grant her divorce and her rights (spousal support and custody of children), does she deserve her full spousal rights?

Answer: The wife mentioned above does not deserve the spousal maintenance from a *shari'a* point of view. But her *mahr* (dowry) and her right of custody of children (under the age of two) are not suspended because of her disobedience.

442. Question: A young lady had gone through an operation in which her womb was removed, and consequently she had stopped experiencing her menses for more than fifteen years. Then she marries a man in temporary marriage for a length of time that has now ended. Is it necessary for her to observe the waiting period *('idda)*? And if yes, then what would be the time length of her *'idda*?

Answer: If she still is in the age of women who usually see their menses, then her *'idda* in the temporary marriage would be forty-five days.

443. Question: Sometimes a non-Muslim woman would verbally bear witness [of belief in Islam] for the sake of marriage which does attract plausible considerable credence for others that she has really believed in Islam. Can the others [who have doubts about her belief] still treat with her as they would treat Muslims?

Answer: Yes, the Islamic treatment would be applied to her as long as she does not say or do something that would contradict [her declaration of the faith].

444. Question: Sometimes the fertilized ovum of a woman is transplanted in the womb of another woman. Is this allowed? If pregnancy occurs, whose child will this foetus be considered?

Answer: There is no problem as long as the *harãm* touching and looking is not involved. And whether the genealogical mother of the child will be the genetic mother (who provided the ovum) or the biological mother (who carried the foetus in her womb), there are two views. Based on obligatory precaution, caution should be exercised in regard to both of them.

445. Question: The foetus swims in the liquid that is in the mother's womb. This liquid comes out at the time of birth or just before it, sometimes with blood, at other times without blood. Is this water to be considered ritually pure if it comes out without blood?

Answer: Yes, it is ritually pure *(tãhir)* in this case.

446. Question: When is it permissible to abort a feotus? Does the age of the foetus have anything to do with it?

Answer: Abortion is not allowed after the implantation of the [fertilized] ovum [on the lining of the womb] except if the mother's life is in danger or the continuation of pregnancy will cause difficulty for her that is not normally bearable and there is no other solution but abortion. In this case, it would be permissible to abort the foetus as long as the soul has not entered into it; after the entering of the soul, it is not permissible at all.

447. Question: Sometimes the doctors reach the following conclusion: This foetus is afflicted with a very serious disease; it is therefore preferable that it should be aborted because if that child is born, it will be deformed or will die soon after birth. Is it, therefore, permissible for the doctor to abort the foetus? Is it permissible for the mother to agree to the abortion? And who of the two will become liable for indemnity?

Answer: Just the fact that the child will be deformed or that it will not live for a long time after his birth does not ever justify that pregnancy be terminated. Therefore, it is not permissible for the mother to consent to the abortion just as it is not permissible for the doctor to go ahead with the procedure. And whoever performs the abortion will become liable for the indemnity.

448. Question: Is a mother allowed to abort her feotus if she does not want it while the soul has not yet entered it and there is no serious danger to the mother's life?

Answer: She is not allowed to do that, except if the continuation of the pregnancy will cause harm to her health or put her in an unbearable difficulty.

* * *

Chapter Eight

WOMEN'S ISSUES

Introduction

There are specific laws for women in Islam that the books of jurisprudence have discussed in detail. However, as a result of being in the midsts of non-Muslim societies, new situations have come up that have given rise to new questions and inquiries.

General Rules

449. A woman is allowed to keep her **face and hands** uncovered in the presence of a non-*mahram* man, provided that she does not fear of getting into a *harām* act, that the exposure of her face and hand does not cause men to gaze at her in a forbidden way, and that it does not give rise to immorality in general. Otherwise, it is obligatory on her to conceal [her face and hands] even from those who are *mahram* to her.

450. It is not permissible for a woman to expose the top part of her **feet** to a non-*mahram* onlooker. However, she is allowed to keep her feet —top as well as sole— exposed during salāt, if she is in a place where she is immune from the looks of a non-*mahram* person.

451. A woman is allowed to put **kohl** on her eyelashes and to wear **rings** in both hands, provided that it is not intended for drawing lustful attention of men towards herself and that she is confident of not getting into a harām act. Otherwise, it is obligatory upon her to cover [the eyes that have kohl and the hands with rings] even from those who are *mahram* to her.

452. It is permissible for a woman to go out, wearing perfume even if non-*mahram* men can smell her **perfume**; however, this should not lead to those men becoming attracted to her and that her purpose in wearing perfume was not to arouse or attract men.

453. It is permissible for a woman to ride in a car by herself with a non-*mahram* driver as long as she is confident of not getting into a harām act.

454. It is not permissible for a woman to masturbate until she reaches climax and has discharge. If she did so, it is obligatory upon her to perform the major ablution *(ghusl)*; and this *ghusl* will make up for *wudhu* [if she intends to pray after that].

455. A woman who is afflicted with barrenness is permitted to expose her private parts [to the doctor] for the sake of treatment if she desperately needs to become pregnant and that failure to do so would place her in a difficulty of the kind that would exempt her from other obligations.

456. "The baby should be **breast fed** by its mother because it has been mentioned in ahādíth that, 'There is no milk that a child drinks more blessed than the milk of his mother.' It is better to breast feed the child for twenty-one months; it should not be less than that. Similarly, the child should not be breast fed for more than two years; it is better if the parents agree on weaning the child earlier."[131]

457. It is recommended for the wife to do the **household chores** and to provide the needs of the husband unrelated to conjugal matters like cooking, sewing, cleaning, laundry, etc. These things are not an obligation on her.

458. "It is permissible to **listen to** the voice of a non-*mahram* woman without any sexual overtures.

"Similarly, it is permissible for her to make herself be heard by non-*mahram* men except when there is fear of getting into a harām act. However, she is not allowed to soften or make her voice palatable to an extent that would normally arouse the listener even if that person was *mahram* to her."[132]

459. "If a woman is in need of medical examination to treat her disease and the non-*mahram* doctor is better equipped to treat her, that doctor is allowed to look at her body and touch it if need be. If it is possible to treat her by either of the two methods (looking or touching), he [should restrict himself to one and] would not be allowed to use the other [method]."[133]

460. Some scholars say, "In order to confine all kinds of sexual activity to wedlock and for the benefit of the husband, the wife and the entire family, Islam has imposed *hijāb* on the woman when she meets the men who are not *mahram* to her."[134]

461. Alfred Hitchcock, the famous movie producer said, "The eastern woman was very attractive by herself and this attraction gave her tremendous power. But by taking great steps in getting herself at a par with her western sister, the

---

[131] Sayyid as-Sistāni, *Minhāju 's-Sāliheen,* vol. 3, p. 120.
[132] Ibid, p. 15.
[133] Ibid, p. 13.
[134] See Shaykh Murtaza Mutahhari, *Masalatu 'l-Hijāb* as quoted in the first issue of *al-Kawthar,* p. 92.

eastern woman has gradually abandoned the hijāb; and this has gradually decreased her attractiveness [and hence her power]."[135]

462. Will Durant, while discussing the sexual behaviour of women, said, "The woman knows that indecency leads to lower self-esteem and degradation, therefore she taught that to her daughter."[136] In other words, she by nature is inclined towards decency and chastity; and that covering her body increases her honour and position in the eyes of men.

Questions and Answers

463. **Question:** What is the ruling on a woman embracing another woman passionately, kissing, and flirting with her with sexual desire? What if they go even further and enter the limit of deviant sexual behaviour?

Answer: All of this is harām with varying degrees of prohibition.

464. **Question:** Very often women ask specific questions [related to women's issues] from theology students. Is it permissible for them to ask explicitly even though some questions might be of a private nature? Is it permissible for the student to answer them in the same explicit manner?

Answer: It is permissible for both parties for the sake of learning and teaching religious laws, but they both must have sincerity of intention, observe decency and decorum [in their

---

[135] See *al-Kawthar;* [Translator's Note: The quotation has been translated from Arabic. Original source not traceable.]

[136] Translator's Note: Translated from Arabic. Orignal source not traceable.

speech], and refrain from explicitness in matters that are not appropriate to be expressed explicitly.

465. Question: During foreplay, a sticky substance is discharged in the woman's vagina; and when the foreplay continues, she sometimes has orgasm. Is it obligatory on her to do the major ablution *(ghusl)* when she reaches the first stage of discharge or only when she reaches the climax? And will this ghusl make up for *wudhu*?

Answer: The major ablution *(ghusl)* does not become wājib for the woman until she reaches the level of sexual excitement. Once she reaches that level and the liquid is discharged from her, it becomes obligatory on her to perform ghusl of *janābat* and that compensates for *wudhu*.

466. Question: During the pilgrimage season, women use some pills to delay their monthly period; when the period sets in, it comes with frequent intervals. Would the laws of menses apply on that discharge?

Answer: If it comes with interruption and does not continue —even inside the private part after the first initial discharge— for three days, the laws of menstruation should not apply.

467. Question: A vast majority of Muslim women who observe *hijāb* are used to keeping their chins and a small part of the under chin exposed but they cover the neck. Is this permissible for them? And how big an area of the face women can expose; are the ears included in that?

Answer: The ears are not part of the face, therefore it is obligatory to cover them. As for the part of the chin and the under chin that is seen when putting on the common head scarf, it is to be considered as part of the face.

468. Question: Is it permissible to shake hands with a non-*mahram* women advanced in age *(qawā'id)* who do not have high hopes of getting married? What is the approximate age for *qawā'id*?

Answer: It is not permissible to touch the body of a non-*mahram* woman at all, except when necessary. There is no specific age for the *qawa'id* because it varies from one woman to another; the criterion [of defining the *qawā'id*] is what has been mentioned in the [Qur'ānic] verse: she should be advanced in age and do not aspire for marriage (24/60).

469. Question: If putting on the face veil *(an-niqāb)* in a country [like England or America] sometimes arouses astonishment and inquiries, is it obligatory to take off such veil since it would become part of the *libāsu 'sh-shuhra*?

Answer: It is not obligatory [to do so]. However, if wearing it arouses disapproval by and dislike of the general public in a particular country, it would be classified as *"libāsu 'sh-shuhra"* in that country and it would not be permissible to wear it over there.

470. Question: Is it permissible for a woman in *hijāb* to learn driving if her instructor is a non-*mahram* and alone with her during the driving lessons, provided that nothing harām takes place in that process?

Answer: It is permissible, provided that one is immune from immorality.

471. Question: Some beautician outlets employ female staff. Is it permissible for a woman among the believers to engage in applying make up of women —Muslim or non-Muslim— who do not observe *hijāb* and who wear make up in presence of non-*mahram* men?

Answer: If that work is considered as a contributing factor to the harām act and promoting it, she is not allowed to do it; however, such a consideration is truly far-fetched.

472. Question: Is it permissible for a woman who does not observe *hijāb* to get rid of her facial hair, to straighten her eyebrows, and to wear natural and light make up?

Answer: Getting rid of facial hair and straightening eyebrows do not prevent her from keeping her face open [while putting on the *hijāb*] provided she is confident of not getting into something *harām* and that exposing her face is not with the intention of inviting *harām* looks.

473. Question: Is it permissible [for a woman] to dye her hair, fully or partially, in gatherings exclusively for women with intention of attracting attention for the purpose of marriage?

Answer: If dyeing is for a cosmetic reason and not with the purpose of deceiving (like concealing a defect or old age), there is no problem in it.

474. Question: If a woman puts on a wig that covers her real hair for the purpose of beauty as well as *hijāb,* is she allowed to expose her face now that it looks different?

Answer: She is permitted to use the wig but it is a beauty item that must be concealed from non-*mahram* men.

475. Question: There are some stockings whose colour matches that used to embellish the legs. Is it permissible for a young woman to wear it?

Answer: She is allowed to wear it but if it is considered a beauty item, it is necessary to conceal it from non-*mahram* men.

476. Question: Is it permissible to wear stockings that conceal what is underneath it?

Answer: In principle, there is no problem in it.

477. Question: A Muslim woman works as nurse and visits patients; it is part of her work to touch the body of men, Muslims as well as non-Muslims. Is this permissible for her, knowing that leaving her job would make it hard for her to find work? And is there a difference between touching the body of a Muslim and that of a non-Muslim?

Answer: It is not permissible for a woman to touch the body of non-*mahram* man, Muslim and non-Muslim alike, except when it is necessary, in which case the prohibition is overridden.

478. Question: A Muslim woman wears high heel shoes that hit the ground in such a way that it draws attention. Is she allowed to wear it?

Answer: It is not permissible, if it is intended to draw the attention of non-*mahram* men to herself, or if it generally causes temptation [for committing sin].

479. Question: Is it permissible for a woman to wear rings, bangles, or necklace for the sake of beautification?

Answer: It is permissible and it should be concealed from non-*mahram* men except for the rings and bangles, provided that there is no danger of committing that which is *harām*, or that exposing them should not be with the intention of drawing forbidden attention.

480. Question: In the West it is possible to wear coloured contact lenses. Is it permissible for a Muslim woman to wear them for the sake of beautification and then appear in front of non-*mahram* men?

Answer: If that is considered as an item of cosmetics, it is not allowed.

481. Question: Is it permissible to sell ova of a woman? Is it permissible to buy them?

Answer: It is permissible.

482. Question: In some cases, women start losing their hair. Is it permissible for them to expose their hair to a doctor for the sake of treatment, irrespective of whether loss of hair entails difficulty for them; rather it is just for the sake of embellishment?

Answer: It is permissible in the case of difficulty that is normally unbearable; and not without it.

483. Question: Is it permissible for a Muslim woman to join a co-education college in the West in spite of the moral breakdown, and the laisser-faire attitude of some male and female students?

Answer: If she is confident that she can preserve her faith, fulfill her religious duties, including the *hijāb,* refrain from *harām* looking and touching, and be immune to immoral and misleading atmosphere, there is no problem in it; otherwise, it is not allowed.

484. Question: In some Western countries, artists sit on the kerb of public footpaths and paint pictures of those who wish to get their portraits drawn at a price. They do so by asking their customers to pose for them, and then carefully observe their faces in order to paint their portraits. Is it permissible for a woman with *hijāb* to ask the artist to draw her picture?

Answer: She should not do so.

485. Question: Is wrestling in its various forms permissible for women? And are women allowed to look at the semi-naked bodies of the wrestlers live or on television without lustful thoughts?

Answer: Wrestling is not allowed if it involves hurting oneself or the opponent when it crosses the boundary of haram. It is a compulsory obligation for a woman not to look at the body of a man, innocently, even on television, with the exception of the head, hands and feet, and other parts that are not normally concealed.

486. Question: Is it permissible for women to look at the bodies of men who take off their clothes [i.e., shirts] during the mourning ceremony [when they do the *mātam*]?

Answer: Based on obligatory precaution, they should refrain from it.

487. Question: A man voluntarily takes the responsibility of raising a girl, then she grows up into a woman. Is it obligatory on her to observe *hijāb* in his presence? Is it obligatory on him not to look at her hair and not to touch her at all?

Answer: Yes, all that is obligatory; and her relations with him should be like that of a non-*mahram*.

488. Question: If pregnancy causes great difficulty for a daughter and a disgrace for her family, is she allowed to abort the foetus?

Answer: It is permissible before the soul enters the feotus, if the difficulty reaches a level that is usually unbearable and there is no way out for her except abortion.

489. Question: Is a woman allowed to wear trousers and go out on the streets and markets?

Answer: It is not allowed if it reveals the contours of her body or would normally arouse temptation.

490. Question: Is it permissible to wear a wig with the purpose of drawing attention and embellishing oneself in gatherings that are exclusively for women? Is this counted as "concealing the shortcomings"?

Answer: There is no problem in it, if it is done only for beautification, and not for deceiving and concealing physical shortcomings, in the case of would-be marriage.

491. Question: Is it permissible for a woman in menses to recite more than seven verses from the Holy Qur'ān (other than the verses of obligatory prostration)? If that it is permissible, is it disliked *(makrûh)?* And does that mean that she will be rewarded for reciting, albeit less [than normal]?

Answer: She is allowed to recite other than the verses that require obligatory prostration; and when it is said, "it is disliked to recite more than seven verses," this means that the reward of such recitation will be less.

* * *

Chapter Nine

YOUTHS' ISSUES

Introduction

The influx of devout Muslim youths to the non-Muslim countries has increased, especially in European and American countries where they come for education, temporary visits, or for permanent residence.

The commitment of Muslim youths to Islam causes great concerns, problems, and inquires about the issues that are important to them. Therefore it is appropriate to present the following religious laws which address some of these concerns. (See the question-answer section below.)

General Rules

492. The mujtahids talk about prohibition of **looking indecently and lustfully at women**. By the expression "prohibition of looking lustfully," they mean that it is prohibited to look at them with sexual desire. By the expression "looking indecently," they mean a glance that could lead one to a situation whereby they may be tempted to commit a harãm act.

493. It is permissible to look without lust at the women who would not listen if they were forbidden from exposing themselves [by not observing the *hijāb*]. Therefore, it is permissible to look at the face, the hands, and the feet of the woman as well as those parts of their bodies that they normally expose in public but not those parts that some of them, against their own custom, would expose publicly. This is with the condition that the look is not combined with carnal appetite and the onlooker should not fear of getting into a situation of committing the *harām*. (See the question-answer section below and issue No. 500).

494. It is not permissible for a man to look at another man with lust; similarly, it is not permissible for a woman to look at another woman with lust.

495. Homosexuality *Ash-shudhûdh al-jinsi* is harām. Similarly, it is forbidden for a female to engage in sexual act with another female, i.e. lesbianism. (See the question-answer section below.)

496. Masturbation by any means whatsoever is forbidden; this is sometimes known as "secret habit — *al-'ādatus sirriya*".

497. Based on obligatory precaution, one must refrain from viewing **pornographic pictures** and films, even if one looks at them without indecent intention and lust. (See the question-answer section below.)

498. The immoral establishments have produced an item that has the features of the private parts of a woman, and it is possible for a man to become intimate with it by placing it over his penis at bedtime. Based on obligatory precaution, one must refrain from using it even if he does not intend to reach the stage of discharge. This law applies without any difference to the married as well as the unmarried man. (See the question-answer section below.)

499. It is permissible for man to use **condoms** to prevent pregnancy; however, it is precautionarily obligatory that he should seek the consent of his wife in using the condom.

500. It is not permissible for a Muslim man to go to unisex **swimming** pools and other places where people go about half-naked if it entails a *harām* act. Based on obligatory precaution, one must refrain from going to such places even if it does not entail a *harām* act.

501. A Muslim man is not allowed to **shake hands** of a woman without a barrier like gloves unless refraining from shaking hands will put him in a considerable harm or unbearable difficulty. In the latter case, he is allowed to shake hands to the extent of necessity only. (See the question-answer section below.)

502. A young man is allowed to kiss his young sister or maternal aunt or paternal aunt or their small daughters out of affection and love. However, he is not allowed to kiss them if that entails sexual arousal.

503. It is *harām* to play **chess** no matter whether the play is with betting or without betting. It is also *harām* to play chess through computerized instrument if there are two players involved in it. Based on obligatory precaution, one must refrain from it even if just the computer is the other player. (See the question-answer section below.)

504. It is similarly *harām* to play with instruments of gambling in which betting is involved. Based on obligatory precaution, one must refrain from it even when no betting is involved.

505. It is permissible to engage in **sports games** with balls like football (soccer), basketball, volleyball, table tennis, handball, etc. It is also permissible to watch such games at the sports stadiums or on various displays and monitors with payment or without payment as long as that does not entail a *harām* act like looking with lust or neglecting an obligation like *salāt*.

506. It is permissible to engage in **wrestling and boxing** without betting as long as it does not lead to serious bodily harm.

507. It is not permissible for a man to **shave** his beard based on obligatory precaution. Similarly, it is not permissible for him to just leave the hair on his chin and shave the sides based on obligatory precaution. (See the question-answer section below.)

508. A Muslim is allowed to shave his beard if he is compelled to do so or if he is forced to shave for medical reasons, etc or if he fears harm to his life by not shaving or if growing the beard would put him in difficulty (for example, if it becomes a cause of his ridicule and humiliation that is not normally tolerable by a Muslim).

Questions and Answers

509. Question: A father asks the friend of his son to monitor the behaviour of his son and then asks him after sometime so that he can know his son's character. Is the friend allowed to disclose the character of the son to the father that might include things that the son does not want to be known to anyone?

Answer: It is not allowed except when his character involves an evil act from which he must be stopped and that stopping him from that is not possible through anything less than uncovering him (which would embarrass and hurt him).

510. Question: What is the meaning of the statement from the *hadīth* that "the first glance is [permissible] for you but the second one will [be held] against you"? Is it permissible to prolong the first glance while looking at a woman on the basis, as claimed by some, that it is still "the first permissible glance"?

Answer: Apparently the meaning of the statement mentioned above is to differentiate between the two glances in the sense that the first was just an accidental and a passing one, and so it is considered guiltless since no lustful desires were involved in it as opposed to the second glance which was naturally intentional and accompanied with an element of desire, and therefore it is detrimental. It is because of this that a statement has been quoted by Imam as-Sãdiq (a.s.) in which he says, "The glance after the [first] glance creates in the heart the desire and that is sufficient as a temptation for the person."

It is however clear that the statement quoted in the question does not intend to define the permissible glance on basis of numbers in the sense that the first glance is permissible even if it is intentional and guileful from the very beginning. Or that it becomes such if it is prolonged and continues because the on-looker cannot control by casting his glance away from woman that he is looking at. Neither does it mean that the second glance is forbidden even if it is for a single moment without any lust at all.

511. Question: While discussing the issue of looking at a woman, many expressions are used that are not clearly defined for most people. So what is the meaning of "*ar-rayba, at-taladh-dhudh,* and *ash-shahwa*"?

Answer: *At-Taladh-dhudh* and *ash-shahwa* mean lustful and sexual desire, not just any lust or any desire that is part of the human instinct that appears when one sees beautiful scenes.

Ar-rayba means the fear of temptation or of falling into haram.

512. Question: What is the limit of forbidden lust?

Answer: Its minimum limit —if what is meant is the ranking order— i.e. it is the first stage of sexual arousal.

513. Question: In British government schools and also in other Western countries the students, male as well as females, are taught sex education which includes detailed description of sexual organs with models or without them. Is it permissible for a young student to attend classes like this? Is it necessary for the parents to prevent the young child from attending such classes when the child expresses interest in it by claiming that it will be useful for him in the future?

Answer: If attending such classes does not entail other *harām* deeds like looking lustfully and, as a result of studying that unit, he will be prevented from deviant behaviour, then there is no problem in it.

514. Question: Is it permissible to recite erotic poems in presence of women without intending to woo them or with such an intention if they are unmarried and can be influenced by such recitation?

Answer: This is not allowed.

515. Question: Is it permissible to talk to women about love without lustful intention or fear of temptation or encouraging a *harām* act?

Answer: Based on obligatory precaution, it is not allowed.

516. Question: Is it permissible to praise in erotic poetry or in prose a unspecified woman or women in general?

Answer: If it is devoid of intent to commit *harām* or similar acts and entails no other harm [in moral and ethical sense], then there is no problem in it.

517. Question: Is it permissible to talk with women without lustful intention for the purpose of gaining satisfaction with one of them and then to propose temporary marriage to her?

Answer: If the talk is devoid of what one should be talking about to a strange [i.e., non-*mahram*] woman, then there is no problem in it.

518. Question: A new craze has spread in Europe in which men wear ladies' earrings in one or both ears. Is this allowed for them?

Answer: It is not permissible if it is made of gold; rather not at all, based on obligatory precaution.

519. Question: If a person commits *harām* by shaving his beard by razor on day one, then is it permissible for him to use the razor the second, the third, the fourth day and so on?

Answer: It is precautionarily compulsory to refrain from it.

520. Question: At times the big companies in Europe discriminate —among those who come to them seeking job— between those who shave the beard and those who don't shave it. If this is true, then is it permissible to be clean shaven in order to get the job?

Answer: Shaving the beard —whose prohibition is based on obligatory precaution— would not become permissible just by the desire to get a job with these companies.

521. Question: Is it permissible to shave the two sides of the face and leave the hair on the chin?

Answer: Shaving the beard is haram based on obligatory precaution, and this includes the hair that grows on the sides of the face. However, there is no problem in shaving the hair that grows on the cheeks.

522. Question: Is it permissible to play games of chance of all kinds on electronic machines (computers) without betting or with betting?

Answer: It is not permissible, and it is treated same as normal [non-electronic] gambling instruments.

523. Question: Some permissible games use dice in them. So is it allowed to play with it?

Answer: If the dice is not from the tools that are exclusively for gambling, then there is no problem in using it in non-gambling games.

524. Question: Is it permissible to look at what the non-Muslim women normally expose of their body during the summer season?

Answer: If the glance does not entail lustful desire or temptation [to commit sins], then there is no problem in it.

525. Question: Is it permissible to look at the picture of a well-known *muhajjaba* woman who appears without hijāb in that picture? [*Muhajjaba* means a lady who observes *hijāb*.]

Answer: Based on obligatory precaution, one must refrain from looking at other than the face and the hands of that woman; even in the case of these two, it is permissible without lustful intent and temptation [for sin].

526. Question: (a) Is it permissible to look at non-Muslim women who are naked or half-naked in television and its like for the purpose of fulfilling the inquisitive nature with no guarantee whether or not sexual desire will be aroused?

(b) Is it permissible to look at them in the streets not for the purpose mentioned above but for arousing [the sexual desire of] the husband towards his wife?

Answer: It is not permissible to look with lust at the naked live scenes or on the television and etc. Rather, based on compulsory precaution, one must refrain from it at all times.

527. Question: Is it permissible to look at arousing scenes with confidence in not attaining arousal?

Answer: If it is a naked [indecent] scene, then based on obligatory precaution, one should refrain from looking at it.

528. Question: Is it permissible to view sex movies without lust?

Answer: It is not permissible at all based on obligatory precaution.

529. Question: There are certain television stations that offer monthly subscription for their programs that are not of immoral nature; but after midnight, it relays sexual movies. Is it permissible to subscribe in such programs?

Answer: It is not allowed unless one is confident about himself and others [in the house] that they would not view the sexual shows.

530. Question: In some countries it is customary that the person who arrives [at a meeting or an office] will shake hand with all who are present including women, of course, without lustful intention. And if he refuses to shake hands with the women, it would be considered abnormal and more often than not it would be considered an act of contempt and insult towards the woman. All this would reflect negatively on their view concerning him. Is it therefore permissible to shake hands with women?

Answer: It is not permissible. And the problem should be tackled by not shaking the hands of anyone or by wearing gloves, for example. If this is not possible for him and he thinks that refusing to shake hands would cause great and unbearable difficulty for him, then it is permissible at that time. All this is based on the assumption that it is necessary for him to attend such a gathering; otherwise, if it is not possible for him to refrain from harām, then it is not permissible for him to attend such a gathering.

531. Question: In Western countries, shaking hands is considered as a means of greeting and salutation. Refraining from it could sometimes lead to deprivation from job and education opportunities. So is it permissible for a Muslim man to the shake hand of a woman or for a Muslim woman to shake the hand of a man in necessary circumstances?

Answer: When refraining from touching is not possible by wearing gloves or something like it, then it is permissible if not shaking hands would lead to considerable harm or great difficulty that is normally unbearable.

532. Question: Is it permissible for a Muslim man who resides in the West to marry non-Muslim women when Muslim women are scarce in spite of the dangers that exists in regard to children because of difference in language, religion, ways of upbringing children, values, and social customs — all this could lead to psychological problems for the children?

Answer: It is not permissible for him to marry a woman from Ahlul Kitab on a permanent basis.

Although temporary marriage is permissible, we advise him not to have children through her. This applies if he does not already have a Muslim wife even if she is away from him, and in this case it would not be permissible without her consent—rather even with her consent [it is not permissible] based on obligatory precaution.

533. Question: Some companies have produced an item similar to the woman's vagina that some men would place over their penis at bedtime for carnal desire. Is this classified as the forbidden masturbation?

Answer: It is harām if he seeks to ejaculate intentionally or ejaculation is normal [in such a circumstance] for him. Rather, based on obligatory precaution, he must refrain from it even if he is confident of not ejaculating.

534. Question: What is the ruling on a man embracing another man with lust, and about kissing one another with sexual desire? What if they go even further and enter the limit of deviant sexual behaviour?

Answer: All of this is harām even if there might be difference in the degree of prohibition.

* * *

Chapter Ten

MUSIC, SINGING AND DANCING

Introduction

The residents of non-Muslim countries as well those in some Muslim countries are used to be bombarded by music, songs, and rhythms of dancers be they indoors or outdoors. A question arises in their minds: is it permissible for us to listen to this tune or that song? Is it permissible for us to dance?

I shall answer these two questions and others like them in the following rules.

General Rules

535. Music is an art that has spread far and wide during these days. Some varieties of this art are permissible while others are forbidden; therefore, it is permissible to listen to the first while it is forbidden to listen to the latter.

536. Music that is permissible is the music that does not entail entertainment in gatherings held for that purpose.

Forbidden music is the music that is suitable for entertainment and amusement gatherings.

537. The expression "the music or the song that is suitable for entertainment and amusement gatherings" does not mean that the music or the song's tune amuses the heart or changes the mental state because there is nothing wrong in it. The expression actually means that the person listening to the music or the song's tune —especially if he is an expert in these matters— can distinguish that this tune is used in the entertainment and amusement gatherings or that it is similar to the tunes used therein. (See the question-answer section below.)

538. It is permissible to visit places where halāl music is being played, and it is permissible to listen to it as long as it is halāl.

539. It is permissible to visit public places where music is being played even if it is suitable for entertainment and amusement gatherings, provided that one does not intentionally listen to it: for example, the arrival area for passengers, waiting areas for visitors, public parks, restaurants and cafes, etc —even if the music played there is suitable for entertainment and amusement gatherings— because there is no problem in hearing forbidden tunes without intending to listen to it.

540. It is permissible for adults as well as children to learn the art of halāl music in music schools or other places as long as their visits to such places do not have any negative effect on their proper upbringing.

541. Singing *(al-ghinā')* is harām: doing it, listening to it, or living of it. By "singing — *al-ghinā'*," I mean an amusing statement expressed in the tunes that are suitable for those who provide entertainment and amusement.

542. It is not permissible to recite the Holy Qur'ān, supplications (*du'ā*s), and words of praise in tunes that are commensurate to entertainment and amusement gatherings.

Based on obligatory precaution, one must refrain from reciting other non-amusing statements, in poetry or prose, in that tune. (See the question-answer section below.)

543. The prohibition of intentionally listening and giving ear to harām songs and music has come in the holy tradition. The Messenger of Allāh (s.a.w.) said, "And the person with the [sin of] song *(al-ghinā')* will be raised [on the day of resurrection] blind, deaf and dumb. The person with [the sin of] adultery, of wood-wind, and of drum will also be raised in the same way."[137]

He also said, "Whoever listens to the entertainment (song and music), lead will be melted inside his ear on the day of judgement."[138] He also said, "Singing and music are enchantment for adultery."[139] That is, it is a stepping stone or a way that leads to adultery.

544. It is permissible for a woman to **dance** in front of her husband to please and arouse him. But it is not permissible for her to dance in front of other men; based on obligatory precaution, she must not dance in front of other women also. (See the question-answer section below.)

545. It is permissible to **applaud** in a marriage ceremony, religious gatherings, seminars, and other functions. This is equally permissible for women and men.

---

[137] As-Sayyid al-Khu'I, *al-Masā'ilu 'sh-Shar'iyya,* vol. 2, p. 22.
[138] Ibid.
[139] Ibid, p. 23.

Questions and Answers

546. Question: Many questions are asked concerning permissible and forbidden music.

Is it correct to say that the music that arouses sexual, lustful urges and promotes unstable and degrading behaviour is the forbidden one?

And is it correct to say that the music that soothes the nerves or causes relaxation, the music that forms the background of a scene in a movie to increase the effect of the scene on the viewers, the music that is used for physical exercise during the workouts, the music that dramatizes a particular scene by its tune, or the one that arouses the zeal [in soldiers] is the permissible one?

Answer: Forbidden music is the music that is suitable for entertainment and amusement gatherings, even if it does not arouse sexual temptations.

Permissible music is the music that is not suitable for such gatherings, even if it does not soothe the nerves like the martial music and that played at funerals.

547. Question: Just as many questions are asked about halāl and harām music, many questions are asked about halāl and harām songs.

Is it correct to say that harām songs are those that arouse sexual, lustful urges and promote unstable and degrading behaviour?

Is it correct to say that songs that do not arouse lustful desires, but elevate the souls and thoughts to lofty levels like religious songs of praise dedicated to the Prophet Muhammad (s.a.w.) and the Imams (a.s.), or the songs that lift the spirits and morale [of the fighters] and others like those are halāl songs?

Answer: All songs *(al-ghinā')* are harām. Based on the definition that we accept, *al-ghinā'* is the entertaining expression by way of tunes that are common to those who provide entertainment and amusement.

In this prohibition, we should include the recitation of the Holy Qur'ān, supplications *(du'ās)*, and songs of praise of Ahlul Bayt (a.s.) uttered to the accompaniment of those tunes [that are used by the entertainers]. The prohibition of reciting other non-entertaining expressions —like songs intended to lift the morale [of fighters]— is based on compulsory precaution.

However, the tune that cannot be described as such is not harām by itself.

548. Question: Is it permissible to listen to religious songs in praise of Ahlul Bayt (a.s.) that are accompanied with music?

Answer: Songs *(al-ghinā')* are harām absolutely. However, the praises [of the Prophet or the Ahlul Bayt] that are sung with a good tune but are not in *ghinā'* form are without problem.

As for the music, it would be allowed if it is not suitable for entertainment and amusement gatherings.

549. Question: Is it permissible to soothe the senses by listening to the reciter of the Qur'ān who recites in a vibrant, quavering tone?

Answer: If the tune used in its recitation is not *ghinā'*, there is no problem in listening to it.

550. Question: Some of the reciters, singers or chanters adopt the tunes of sinful people [i.e., harām entertainers] and then sing or chant with their tunes poems in praise of the Prophet (s.a.w.) and his family—the result is that the context is different from that of the sinful people, yet the tune is suitable to theirs. Is it forbidden to sing in this way? Is it forbidden to listen [in this case]?

Answer: Yes, it is forbidden based on obligatory precaution.

551. Question: Is it permissible for the women to sing on the eve of marriage in any tune whatsoever even if it is suitable for the gatherings of sinful people? Is it permissible for them to use musical instruments while singing that night? Is it permissible for them to sing in the wedding ceremony or on its eve wearing henna [on the bride's hand and feet], or on the eve of the seventh night [after the marriage]? Or is the permission restricted to the marriage eve?

Answer: Based on compulsory precaution, they should refrain from it, even on marriage eve, let alone other occasions. As for the issue of music, its rules have already been mentioned earlier.

552. Question: Is it permissible to listen to revolutionary songs accompanied by sounds of piano, lute, drum, wind-pipe, and electronic piano?

Answer: If the music accompanying it is that which is suitable for entertainment and amusement gatherings, it is not permissible to listen to it.

553. Question: What is the meaning of the terminology: "common among sinful people"?

Answer: This expression is not mentioned in our fatwas (religious edicts). What we have mentioned in defining *al-ghinā'* is "the tunes that are common for those who provide entertainment and amusement;" and its meaning is clear.

554. Question: A non-practicing Muslim has recently become more committed [to Islam]. Is it permissible for him to softly hum what he remembers from the past songs by himself or in front of his friends?

Answer: If it falls in the category of *al-ghinā'*, then it is not allowed.

555. Question: There are certain songs in foreign languages that the teachers of linguistics recommend listening to in order to expedite the learning of that language. Is it permissible to listen to such songs for that purpose?

Answer: If it falls within the category of *al-ghinā'* as explained earlier, it is not allowed.

556. Question: Musical instruments are of different kinds. Sometimes they are used in musical gatherings and sometimes for soothing the soul. Is it then permissible to buy these instruments, manufacture them, deal in them, or play them to soothe the soul or listen to the music when someone else is playing them?

Answer: It is not permissible to deal in the instruments of harām entertainment: neither selling nor buying or etc. just as it is not permissible to manufacture them and accept remuneration for making them.

"Instrument of harām entertainment" means that its physical shape—that gives its value and eventually the purpose for waiting to acquire it— is not suitable except for use in harām entertainment.

557. Question: Is it permissible to manufacture, sell, or buy musical instruments that are made for children's play? And is it permissible for adults to use them?

Answer: If the music that is suitable for entertainment and amusement gatherings comes out of it, then it is neither permissible to deal in, nor are adults allowed to use them.

558. Question: In government schools of the United Kingdom and may be some other countries also, students have to take part in dance classes to the sound of special musical tunes that synchronize the movements of the students while they are dancing.

(a) Is it permissible to attend such classes?

(b) Is it obligatory on the parents to prevent their children from attending such classes if the young boy or girl is inclined towards attending them?

Answer: (a) It is not permitted if it has any negative effect —which is quite common— on their religious upbringing. Rather, it is not permitted at all, as a matter of obligatory precaution.

(b) Yes, it is obligatory. Also please consult the answer to question no. 563 below.

559. Question: Is it permissible to learn dancing?

Answer: It is not allowed at all, as a matter of obligatory precaution.

560. Question: Is it permissible to organize dance parties where each husband dances only with his own wife to the sound of soothing musical tunes, wearing dresses that are not indecent?

Answer: It is not allowed.

561. Question: Is it permissible for women to dance in front of other women or for men to dance in front of other men in a gender-wise segregated gathering with or without music?

Answer: Dancing of women in front of women or dancing of men in front of men is a problematic case; as a matter of obligatory precaution, one must refrain from it. The rules governing music have already been discussed earlier.

562. Question: Is it permissible for a wife to dance for her husband with music or without music?

Answer: It is allowed as long as dancing is not accompanied with harām music.

563. Question: Some schools in the West force their male and female students to learn dancing. This dancing is neither accompanied by the common song nor is it for entertainment; it is part of the educational curriculum. So, is it harām for parents to allow their sons and daughters to attend such classes?

Answer: Yes, if it is contravenes the religious upbringing. Rather it is, based on obligatory precaution, forbidden absolutely, if the student has reached the age of maturity — except if he has a valid reason for approving it; for example, if he follows a *mujtahid* who allows it. In the latter case, nothing prevents him from allowing his child to take part in [such activity].

* * *

```
┌─────────────────────────────────┐
│                                 │
│        Chapter Eleven           │
│                                 │
│       MISCELLANEOUS             │
│                                 │
└─────────────────────────────────┘
```

Introduction

The respected reader will find in this chapter some laws, questions and answers related to a variety of important issues that could not easily be classified under one or the other of the previous chapters, hence the "Miscellaneous" title.

General Rules

564. It is recommended to **give children** names that reflect servitude towards the Almighty Allāh [for example, 'Abdullāh; 'Abdur Rahmān; 'Abdur Rahím] just as it is recommended to name them by the name of the Prophet Muhammad (s.a.w.), and the other Prophets and Messengers (a.s.). It is recommended to name the children as 'Ali, Hasan, Husayn, Ja'far, Tālib, Hamza, and Fātima.

And it is disliked to give them names of the enemies of Islam and Ahlul Bayt (a.s.).

565. The **custody**, upbringing, and care of the child whether male or female for the first two *hijri* [lunar] years is the right of both parents equally. Therefore, it is not permissible for the father to separate the child from its mother during these two years.

When these two years come to an end, the right of custody is the father's alone. However, based on precaution, it is recommended that the father should not separate the child from its mother until he or she reaches the age of seven.

566. If the parents separate because of annulment or divorce before the child —whether male or female— reaches the age of two (by *hijri* account), the mother does not lose the right of custody of the child as long as she does not marry another man. Therefore, it is necessary for both parents to agree on exercising their common right in custody by alternating [the right] or by any other method on which both agree.

567. If the mother marries after separating from the father, she forfeits her right of custody, and the custody will be the exclusive right of the father.

568. The term of custody ends when the child reaches the age of mental maturity. When the child reaches mental maturity, no one has the right of custody over him or her, not even the parents let alone others. The child, then becomes independent in his affairs; and so he can choose to join either of the two parents or anyone besides them. However, if his separation from both of them causes distress to them out of their concern for him or her, it is not permissible for the child to disobey them in that matter. If the father and the mother differ [in the case of distress], the priority is given to the mother.

569. When the father dies, the mother has greater right of custody than anyone else until the child reaches the age of maturity.

570. When the mother dies during the term of her custody, the father gets the exclusive custody.

571. Just as custody is a right of the father and the mother, it is also the right of the child in the sense that if they refuse to take the custody [and fulfill their duties towards him], they can be forced to comply.

572. If both parents disappear, the right of custody belongs to the paternal grandfather.

573. Whoever from the two parents or others have the right of custody is allowed to delegate it to a third party, ensuring that they would fulfill their responsibility as required by Islamic Law.

574. The person —parents or others— who shall have the custody of the child, must be Muslim, sane, and trustworthy with regard to the safety of the child. So if the father is a non-Muslim and the mother is a Muslim, the child is considered as a Muslim and the mother shall have the sole custody of the child. Similarly, if the father is a Muslim while the mother is a non-Muslim, the father shall have the right of custody.

575. It is obligatory upon the son **to provide** for the parents.

576. It is obligatory upon the father to provide for the child, male as well as female.

577. The obligation of providing for a person who is closely related to you is conditional on him being poor, in the sense that he does not have the basic necessities for his life like bread, food, clothing, bedding, comforter, shelter, etc.

578. In Islamic law, there is no fixed amount for providing to those who are closely related to you. What is obligatory is to provide whatever is needed to sustain him, i.e. bread, food, clothing, shelter, and other things by considering his status as well as the standard of living for that place and time.

579. If a person who is obliged to provide for the needs of his close relation refuses to provide [e.g., a husband refuses to provide for his wife], it is permissible for the one who has the right to force him to provide, even by resorting to the courts.

If it is not possible to force him to provide maintenance and he has some wealth [that is easily accessible], the person who has the right can take the rightful amount from it after seeking the permission of the mujtahid.

[And if the wealth of that person who must provide is not easily accessible], the person who has the right can take out a loan in the name of the first person with the permission of the mujtahid. In this case that first person will become liable to pay the loan back. If it is not possible to have recourse to the mujtahid, he should resort to some just [morally upright] believers and take out a loan in the name of the first person who shall then be obliged to repay it.

580. If the protection of the faith and its sacred laws as well as the honour of Muslims and their lands depend on providing for a person or persons from the wealth of Muslims, it is obligatory to do so. In this case, the Muslim who provides will have no right to ask anyone for compensation of what he has spent in this cause.

Questions and Answers

581. **Question:** Is it permissible to draw or produce a scene which shows the Prophet Muhammad (s.a.w.), one of the past prophets or the infallible Imams (a.s.), or sacred historical symbols and show it in cinema, on television or theatre?

Answer: If due deference and respect is observed, and the scene does not contain anything that would detract from their holy pictures in the minds [of the viewers], there is no problem.

582. Question: Is it permissible to give away as gift, copies of the Holy Qur'ān, prayer books, and amulets to non-Muslims?

Answer: There is no problem in it if such is not exposed to desecration and insult, and they are shown the requisite respect.

583. Question: How could one go about dispensing with papers carrying the names of Allāh or the Infallibles, as well as some loose pages of the Qur'ān, when it is not possible for us to throw them in the sea or the river? That said, we do not know where would the garbage end up and what is done with it?

Answer: It is not permissible to put them in rubbish bins because that involves desecration and disrespect. However there is no problem in erasing the writings on the papers even by using some chemicals or burying them in a clean place or shredding them so that it becomes like dust.

584. Question: The way *istikhāra* has become common among us these days—is it mentioned and recommended in the *sharī'a?* Is there a problem in repeating the *istikhāra* [for the same intention] by paying alms [before it] in order to get a guidance that is to one's liking?

Answer: One may resort the *istikhāra* (albeit with the intention of *rajā'an*) in situations where he is confused and cannot prefer one side [of the issue] to the other after having pondered over it and having consulted [those who know about it]. Repeating the istikhara is not right, unless it is a different issue.

585. Question: What is the limit that you have allowed your agents and representatives *(wukalā')* to utilize for their personal use from the religious dues that they collect [from the people]?

Answer: In our *ijāzas* (authorizations for apportioning the religious dues), we have mentioned that the authorized person is allowed to utilize, for example, one-third or half of whatever he collects of religious dues for the purposes that have been defined by the *sharī'a*. This does not mean that the percentage mentioned [in the *ijāza*] is especially for the use of the authorized person himself because it could happen at times that the use of that due would not apply to him at all — for example, if he is a sayyid while the religious dues that he has collected are from the charity of non-sayyid or other charities like it.

In the light of this, if the authorized person considers himself —in keeping with Allāh as the witness in this matter— eligible for the religious dues in accordance with the conditions mentioned in the Manual of Islamic Laws —for example, if he is needy in the religious definition and is among those who deserve the right of *zakāt* or *sihm-e sādāt* or *radd madhālim* etc— he is allowed to take from it according to his need proportionate to his status and not more than that.

Similarly, if he is providing general religious services and strives for upholding the word of Islam, he deserves the *sihm-e* Imām (a.s.) according to the level of his work and the service that he does for Islam.

But if he is not spending the religious due that he has collected, he must utilize the percentage mentioned [in the *ijāza*] in its appropriate causes as defined by the *sharī'a*.

586. Question: If a person has doubts about the integrity of a representative of the *marja'* as a result of alleged misappropriation of religious dues;

(One)   Is he allowed to talk about it to other people even if he is not certain about the truth of the allegations that are against the representative? What if he is certain about it?

(Two)   Is he allowed to still pay his religious dues to that representative as long as he is uncertain about his not being trustworthy?

Answer: (a) It is not permissible for him [to talk to the others about it] in both situations. In the second case [of certainty], he can inform the *marja'* directly in complete confidence about the real situation so that the *marja'* may take whatever actions he deems appropriate.

(b) He should rather pay his religious dues to a representative who is known for his integrity and honesty in acting according to his *ijāza*, i.e. in using some portion of what he has collected of it in their appropriate causes as mentioned earlier and sending the rest to the *marja'*.

587. Question: Is it permissible to use the *sihm-e* Imãm (a.s.) without seeking the permission of the *marja'* if a person can ascertain the need of any kind for its use with which the Imam (a.s.) would be pleased?

Answer: It is not permissible; and one cannot attain the approval of the Imam (a.s.) by using his portion of the khums without seeking the permission of the most learned *marja'* — in that it is possible that the *marja''s* permission is part of the approval of the Imam (a.s.).

588. Question: Is it permissible to use the *sihm-e* Imam (a.s.) in charitable projects while there are tens of thousands of believers who are in need of bread and cloths, etc.?

Answer: In using the *sihm-e* Imam (a.s.), it is important to consider the rule of priorities. It is a matter of obligatory precaution, the determination of "most important *vis-à-vis* the more important" should be left to the discretion of the most learned jurist who is well informed about the general situations.

589. Question: At times while washing the dishes, rice grains go down the drain. Is this allowed? Is it necessary to prevent the rice from going down the drain no matter whether it is more or less, knowing that it is difficult to prevent it?

Answer: It is not permissible to let it go into the drain if it is in an amount that can be used even by feeding the animals. But if it is less or dirty, then it can be put in the dustbin in a way that is not considered an insult, in eyes of the people, to the blessings of Almighty Allāh.

590. Question: Is it permissible for a poet to organize a gathering evening of poetry in which he knows that women without *hijāb* and indecent dress will also attend to listen to his poetry?

Answer: By itself, there is no problem in it; but he must fulfill the duty of enjoining the good and forbidding the evil if the conditions exist.

591. Question: Students are asked to draw a human being or an animal; the requirement is such that it is difficult for the student to refuse the assignment. Are they allowed to do the drawing? What is the ruling if they are asked to do a sculpture work instead of drawing?

Answer: Drawing a non-sculptured figure is allowed. Based on obligatory precaution, it is necessary to refrain from drawing a sculptured picture of a living being. And to say that it is a compulsory part of school work does not justify violating the obligatory precaution. This prohibition is relaxed only in the event of necessity; for example, if not carrying out such an assignment would lead to the student expulsion from the school and that would put him in difficulty of the kind that is normally untolerable.

592. Question: Is it permissible to buy a carving or statue of a totally naked human being, male or female? Is it permissible to buy a carving or statue of an animal and hang it for decoration?

Answer: There is no problem in the second [case of the animal]; as for the first case, if it is [considered a way of] promoting indecency, it is not allowed.

593. Question: Fortune tellers and palmists claim to foretell a person's future. Is it permissible for the palmist to do so if the customer is going to plan [his life] according to his predictions?

Answer: Since the information given by the palmist has no value, it is therefore not permissible for him to give information with certainty just as it is not permissible for the customer to plan according to it, except on legal or reasonable grounds.

593. Question: Is hypnotism permissible? Is invocation of spirits permissible?

Answer: If it puts a person in harm's way, it is harām, and therefore forbidden.

595. Question: Is invocation of jinn with a view to solving the problems of the faithful permissible?

Answer: The same rule mentioned earlier is applicable here.

596. Question: Is cockfighting and bullfighting with permission of their owners allowed?

Answer: It is permissible but disliked as long as it does not cause loss of property.

597. Question: What is the [minimum] limit of the difficulty *(al-haraj)* that lifts the prohibition? Is exorbitant price [for a halāl item] that could still be bought with [financial] strain or by getting a loan a [valid] example that would make a harãm [but cheap alternative] item permissible religiously?

Answer: The circumstances are different in this [case], and the criterion is the extreme hardship that is not normally tolerable.

598. Question: What is the present day equivalent in mithqãl or grams of the weight in gold known as *"al-himsa"*?

Answer: *Al-Himsa* is 1/24 of the *mithqãl as-sayrafi*; and mithqãl as-sayrafi is 4.64 grams; so the weight of al-himsa will be 0.193 grams.

* * *

EPILOGUE

It is important for me to stress at the end of this book that my first attempt in writing *Islamic Laws for Muslims in non-Muslim countries* is in need of evaluation. This being so to establish a body of laws for Muslims in those countries that deal with various aspects of their lives and so that those issues could be governed by noble principles of the Islamic *sharí'a*.

The number of Muslims, be they citizens or residents in non-Muslim countries —especially America and Europe— is increasing. The percentage of the immigrants coming to this part of the world from Muslim lands has also gone up. On the other hand, the pace of change and transformation in these societies is very fast. This on its own poses more questions and creates new situations that must be studied carefully so that the right solutions could be presented. This is needed to keep pace with change in reality, and be proactive rather than reactive.

I should also point out the importance of writing in this subject without loosing sight of spirituality as seen by Islamic ethics and morality, especially in an environment that is attached almost totally to materialism and all that the latter stands for.

I have attempted here and there to emphasize some of Islam's values, as espoused by the Qur'ãnic verses and the noble ahãdíth: This was done in a bid to blend the codes of ethics with jurisprudence just as I have previously done in my book, *al-Fatawal 'l-Muyassara* (Jurisprudence Made Easy) since I have detected the active link between the theoritical and the practical planes [of life]. Also because I can see the need that these teachings should find their way to materialization in the day-to-day conduct of Muslims, especially those who reside in the midst of non-Muslim societies.

It is sufficient for me that I have tried.

I seek the help of Allāh, hope for His aid, and pray for his acceptance since He is the Most Merciful of the Mercifuls. All praise be to Allāh, the Lord of the Universe. And may Allāh be pleased with our master, Muhammad, and his pure and infallible progeny.

The Author.

Terminology Used in the Fatwas

What follows is a list of the some Islamic legal terminology that have been used in the answers of the Respected as-Sayyid as-Sistani (may Allāh prolong his life) to some of the questions of this book:

1. *Al-Ahwat al-awlaa* — more precautionary and better: its significance is the same as that of *al-ihtiyāt al-istihbābi* (# 16 below).
2. *Al-Ahwat luzuuman* — more precautionary and compulsory: its significance is the same as that of *al-ithiyāt al-wujûbi* (# 15 below).
3. *Ãlātu 'l-lahw al-muharram*: the instruments of forbidden entertainment: the tools or instruments that are used exclusively for harām entertainment.
4. *Atrāf shubhati 'l-a'lamiyya* — the group of mujtahids within whom the status of being the *a'lam* (most erudite) is confined. In other words, the group of mujtahids about which we know that one of them is the *a'lam* and that the *a'lam* is not outside that group.
5. *Ad-Dararu 'r-rāfi'atu li 't-taklíf* — the harm that suspends the obligation. A situation of considerable harm or severe difficulty that is not normally tolerable. [Such a situation would supercede other laws.] For example, treatment of a disease which, if left untreated, could lead

to death or loss of limb or an unbearable pain, etc. [— in such a case the treatment must be done even if it violates certain rules of sharí'a].

6. *Dararun mu'tad bih* — considerable harm. A harm from which judicious people would protect themselves like loss or disability of a limb, or severe pain, or loss of considerable wealth.

7. *Ad-Diyah* — indemnity (blood money). The indemnity that has to be paid to the injured party or the heir of the murdered person.

8. *Al-Faskh* — annulment. Cancellation of a contract or a transaction.

9. *Al-Fitnatu 'n-naw'iyya* — general temptation [for harām]. A situation that generally tempts people to commit that which is sinful.

10. *Fi Haddi dhātihi* — by itself; on its own merits. That is, by ignoring other aspects of the issue which might change the original law. For example, it can be said the "on its own demerits, backbiting is forbidden;" but it could be allowed where greater interests are involved like in the case of someone who asks your advice about another person [for giving him employment or accepting his marriage proposal].

11. *Fihi ishkāl* — there is problem in it. The ruling in this case of the same as obligatory precaution.

12. *Fihi ta'ammul* — there is room for reconsideration in it. The ruling in this case is the same as obligatory precaution.

13. *Haqqu 'l-ikhtisās* — the exclusive right. It is a right of a person vis-à-vis an item for which the sharí'a recognizes no ownership or value. For example, wine, pork or meat of an animal not slaughtered according to Islam—the shari'a does recognize the value of these items nor their

ownership for the person who has its possession. However, such a person would have the exclusive right to these items if they were in his possession, for example, a person owned an animal that died [without being slaughtered] or he owned grape juice that formentated and turned into wine. [In such cases, he would have the exclusive right over those items.]

14. *Al-'Idda* — waiting period. The time during which a woman is not allowed to marry after the divorce or the husband's death or after the end of [temporary] marriage or after *wati' bi 'sh-shubha,* etc.

15. *Al-Ihtiyāt al-istihbābi* — precautionary recommendation: This means a precautionary measure recommended by the jurist *(mujtahid)* that his follower *(muqallid)* can ignore.

16. *Al-Ihtiyāt al-wujûbi* — precautionary obligation or an obligation based on precaution: This means a precautionary measure in which the *muqallid* must either follow that opinion of his *mujtahid* or follow the opinion of the second-most learned *mujtahid* in that issue.

17. *Al-Ihrām bi 'n-nadhr* — donning the pilgrim dress *(ihrām)* by making a vow: The pilgrim is not allowed to put on the ihrām except from the *miqāt* (special gateways to the holy territory) or its parallel point. Now if the pilgrim wants to put on the ihrām from a place that is before the miqāt, he is allowed to make a correct religious vow by uttering the required terms. (For example, "In the name of Allāh, I make a vow that I will put on the ihrām from so-and-so city."). This vow must be done before the miqāt or before its parallel point; and then it will be permissible for him to put on the ihrām from that place.

18. *Al-Istihālah* or *taghayyuru 's-surati 'n-naw'iyya* — means the transformation as understood by the common man in the essence of an item that changes into another

item. For example, the flesh in the ground [gradually] changes into dust.

19. *Al-Istihlāk* — annihilation: melting of a matter into another in such a way that it no longer maintains its entity in the eyes of the common people.

20. *Al-Istishāb* — the [principle of] continuity: it means that the previous order or classification would continue in case of a new doubt. [That is, you should act on your previous certainty and ignore your present doubt because doubt cannot over-ride certainty.] For example, if we previously knew that Zayd was a morally upright (*'ādil*) person; and then we see him in a state which creates doubt about his becoming immoral, sinful (*fāsiq*). [In this case, the principle of *istishāb* is applied to] sustain the "previous certainty" against the "present doubt".

21. *Al-Itmi'nān* -- reassurance: the strong conjecture which makes the possibility of its opposite so weak that sensible people would not take it into consideration in their daily lives.

22. *Al-jāhil bi 'l-hukm / al-jāhil bi 'l-mawdu'*— ignorant about the law / ignorant about the application [of that law].

23. "Ignorant about the application" is a person who does not know when is a particular religious law applied in a given case. This could be of two types: Firstly, he does not know the definition of the item on which the law is to be applied — this is known as "shubhatun mafhûmiyya — doubt in defintion of the subject". For example, a person who does not precisely what is meant by the term "ghinā'" [and therefore cannot apply its law]. Secondly, he does not know the identity of the item. For example, he knows the definition of wine but does not know that this particular liquid in a glass on his table is wine or not.

24. *Al-jāhil al-muqassir* — ignorant out of negligence: someone whose ignorance is inexcusable; for example, a person who had the ability to learn but did not bother.

25. *Al-Jāhil al-qāsir* — ignorant out of innocence: someone whose ignorance can be excused; for example, when a person based his action on a legal argument which later on was discovered to be incorrect. So if he asked a question from a religious scholar in whose knowledge and probity he had confidence and later on he discovered that it was a wrong answer, he will be considered to be "*jāhil bi 'l-hukm* — ignorant of the law", yet his ignorance is excuseable in this case.

26. *Al-Jirm al-hā'il* — a film that creates a barrier and prevents the water from reaching the skin.

27. *Al-Kāfir adh-dhimmi:* means a non-Muslim who has made a covenant with the leader of the Muslims; however, there is no real example of this in this day and age.

28. *Al-Kāfir al-mu'āhid:* means a non-Muslim who has made an agreement with Muslims or some Muslims for cease-fire or non-agression.

29. *Al-Kāfir al-muhtaramu 'l-māl:* means a non-Muslim whose property is sacrosanct in Islam. This covers the adh-dhimmi and al-mu'āhid non-Muslim as well as one who has sought asylum with Muslims.

30. *Al-Lihyān:* the two bones on the sides of the face on which the beard grows.

31. *Majhûlu 'l-mālik* — an item whose owner is unknown. This does not apply to an item that the owner has lost.

32. *Mā'u 'l-ghusālah* — the water that has already been used to purify an impure item.

33. *Al-Ma'unatu 's-sanawiyya al-lā'iqah bi 'sh-sha'an* — the annual expenses that are according to his status, that is, his needs and his position in society.

34. *Al-Mashhûr kadhã* — this is what is famous or well-known. This ruling is the same as obligatory precaution.

35. *Ma yalíqu bi sha'nihã bi 'l-qiyãs li zawjihã* means what is appropriate for her status as the wife of her husband.

36. *Al-Milãk* — the criterion: it refers to the benefit and the harm on which religious laws are based.

37. *Al-Mithqãl as-sayrafi:* a weight that is wellknown in the market, especially to the goldsmith [4.64gms.].

38. *Muhãdhãtu 'l-miqãt*: a place that is parrallel to the miqãt (the gateways to the holy territory around Mecca). The criterion is the general perception of being parrallel, it does not have to be scientifically accurate.

39. *Al-Musiqa al-munãsaba li majãlisi 'l-lahw wa 'l-la'ib* — music that is suitable for entertainment and enjoyment gatherings.

40. *Niyyatu 'l-qurbati 'l-mutlaqa* the intention to perform a devotion for seeking nearness to Allãh without mentioning that it is as *adã'* (on time) or *qadhã* (after time), etc.

41. *An-Nushûz*: not respecting the right of other person. It is normally used in case of husband and wife.

42. *Qasdu 'l-badaliyya* — with intention of replacing something with another thing.

43. *Raddu 'l-madhãlim* — the charity given to the needy on behalf of a person who has a monetary right on you but either you cannot idenfy him or reach him or his heirs.

44. *Ash-Shakk* — doubt. Uncertainty in the case where both sides of the issue are equal.

45. *Ash-Shartu 'd-Dimni* and *at-ta'ahhud ad-dimni* — an implied condition / an implied commitment. It means the

condition that is appended to a transaction by common and judicious people, even if it was not explicitly mentioned when the deal took place. For example, we normally say that the value of the price and the merchandise should be compatible to one another. [This is what the common and sensible people understand without really saying it.] Now, if one of the two parties come to know that what he received was less in value than what he paid, for he can claim that he was deceived and cancel the transcation on the basis that the compatiblity of price and commodity is implied by any judicious person.

46. *Ash-Shubha al-mafhûmiyya* — not knowing the application of a term on its materialized reality for lack of knowledge about its definition. For example, we hear a song but are uncertain whether or not the term *al-ghinā'* could be applied on it because we are ignorant of the definition of *al-ghinā'*.

47. *As-Suratu 'l-sanā'iyya al-lati biha qiwāmu 'l-māliyya* — the physical appearance of an item on which its value depends. That is, the particular shape or form of an item for which people would pay money. For example, the shape of a chair or a door or desk: the raw material from which they have been made has a value and its own price but once it was given the shape of the chair or the door then its value is something else.

48. *Tadhkiyya* — is the method of slaughtering of an animal according to Islamic code. This has certain conditions, which makes the eating of the meat of every *halāl* animal which can be normally slaughtered permissible. The flesh and hide of an animal whose meat is forbidden for us become ritually pure (*tāhir*) by *tadhkiyya*.

49. *Tadhkiyya* is of different kinds: (a) In case of fish: 1. taking it out of the water alive; 2. or catching the fish

alive even if it dies thereafter in the net or in the fishing line. (b) In case of land animals by cutting the four blood vessels as in case of sheep, goat, cow, chicken, etc.

50. *At-Tadlís* — deceit, fraud: presenting a person with a quality that does not exist in them in order to attract someone for marriage. Similarly to present an item with a quality that does not exist in it in order to encourage the customer to buy it. For example, if the suitor claims that he belongs to a certain family or that he is a 'sayyid' or holds doctorate degree; or that the lady in that case claims that she was not married before; or if the car-dealer says that the car was never involved in an accident, etc — yet the fact turns out to be otherwise.

51. *At-Taladh-dhudh al-jibilli lil-bashar* — natural feeling of pleasure in humans: the natural pleasure by instincts.

52. *At-Taqsír* in salãt [also *qasr*] — shortening of the prayer: it means the person does the four cylce *(rak'at)* salats in two rak'ats only.

53. *Al-Wali* — the guardian. One who is responsible for the affairs of the child, or of a mentally handicapped person, or of the Muslim society in accordance with Islamic law.

54. *Wati'u 'sh-shubha* means having sexual relation with someone that is not permissible, however, it was done inadvertently thinking that she was his wife or thinking that the marriage was valid (although it was in reality invalid). For example, if a person recites the marriage formula with a woman, has sex with her and then finds out that their marriage was not valid; or that he had sex with a woman in a dark room thinking that she was his wife.

55. *Yajibu 'ala ishkãlin* — for the muqallid, this is same as obligatory. "'Ala ishkãlin" is for the benefit of the mujtahid only.

56. *Yajibu kifāyatan* means it is wãjib on all to do it but if any one does it, the obligation is lifted from all. However, if all fail to do it, then all are responsible.
57. *Yajuzu 'ala ishkāl* — it is permissible to do it; but it is better to refrain based on precaution.
58. *Yajib 'ala ta'ammulin* — for the muqallid, this is same as obligatory. "'Ala tammulin" is for the benefit of the mujtahid only.
59. *Yajuzu 'ala ta'ammulin* — it is permissible to do it; but it is better to refrain from it based on precaution.
60. *Az-Zawāl* — the moment after midday.

* * *

Appendix I

Specimen of the Answers of His Eminence Ayatullah as-Sistãni to some of the questions in this Book

In the name of Allāh, the Beneficent, the Merciful

His Eminence, the Grand Ayatullāh
As-Sayyid 'Ali al-Husyni as-Sistāni (*dāma dhilluh*).

As-Salāmu 'alaykum wa rahmtullāhi wa barakātuh.

I request your kindness in answering the following questions with the hope that the answers would be in simple form that can be understood [easily] by the readers who are not specialist in this science [of Islamic Jurisprudence]. And you shall have an abundance of reward [from the Almighty].

س: يؤجر المسلم في الغرب بيتاً مؤثثاً مفروشاً فهل يستطيع اعتبار كل شيء فيه طاهراً إذا لم يجد أثراً للنجاسة عليه ولو كان الذي يسكنه قبله كتابياً مسيحياً كان أو يهودياً، أو كان بوذياً أو منكراً لوجود الله تعالى ورسله وأنبيائه؟

بسمه تعالى

نعم يستطيع ان بني على طهارة كل شيء يوجد في البيت مالم يعلم او يطمئن بتنجسه ، والظن بالنجاسة لا عبرة به .

س: في أوربا تختلط الديانات والأجناس والألوان فلو اشترينا من صاحب محل يبيع الطعام المبلول ويمسه بيده ونحن لا نعرف دينه فهل نعتبر هذا الطعام طاهراً؟

ان لم نعلم نجاسة يد للناس فالطعام محكوم بالطهارة .

س: بعض الأجبان المصنوعة في الــدول غــير الإســلامية مشتملة على أنفحة العجل أو أي حيوان آخر ولا ندري هل الأنفحة مأخوذة من حيوان منبوح على الطريقة الإسلامية أو لا؟ وهل هي مستحيلة إلى شيء آخر أم لا فهل يجــوز أكل هذه الأجبان؟

لا اشكال في أكل تلك الاجبان من هذه الجهة . والله العالم .

س : ما هي حدود طاعة الأب أو الأم ؟

بسمه تعالى

الواجب على الولد تجاه أبويه أمران :

(الأول) الإحسان إليهما ، بالإحسان عليهما أن كانا محتاجين وتأمين حوائجهما المعيشية وتلبية طلباتهما فيما يرجع إلى شؤون حياتهما في حدود المتعارف والمعقول حسبما تقتضيه الفطرة السليمة ويعد تركها تنكراً لجميلهما عليه ، وهو أمر يختلف سعةً وضيقاً بحسب اختلاف حالهما في القوة والضعف .

(الثاني) مصاحبتهما بالمعروف ، بعدم الإساءة إليهما قولاً أو فعلاً وإن كانا ظالمين له ، وفي البعض (وإن صدر بالـ.... فلا تقهرهما وقل غفر الله لك)

هذا فيما يرجع إلى شؤونهما وأما فيما يرجع إلى شؤون الولد نفسه ما يترتب عليه تأذي أحد أبويه فهو على قسمين :

أ ـ أن يكون تأذيه ناشئاً من شفقته على ولده ، فيحرم التصرف المؤدي إليه سواء نهاه عنه أم لا .

ب ـ أن يكون تأذيه ناشئاً من اتصاف بعض الخصال الذميمة كعدم حبه الخير لولده دينياً كان أم أخروياً ، ولا أثر لتأذي الوالدين إذا كان من هذا القبيل ولا يجب على الولد التسليم لرغباتهما من هذا النوع .

وبذلك يظهر أن الطاعة للوالدين في أوامرهما ونواهيهما الشخصية غير واجبة في حد ذاتها والله العالم . علي الحسيني

س: يتاجر بعض المسلمين بنسخ خطية من القرآن الكريم يجلبونها من البلدان الإسلامية. فهل يجوز ذلك. وإذا كـان المانع منه حرمة بيع القرآن للكافر فهل يجوز التحلل مـن هذا القيد لتصح المعاملة؟ وعلى فـرض الجـواز فكيـف نتحلل من هذا القيد؟

بسمه تعالى

لا نرخص في ذلك من حيث كونه إضراراً بثروات المسلمين وذخائرهم.

س: هل يجوز الشراء من محـلات تخصـص بعضـا مـن أرباحها لدعم إسرائيل؟

لا يجوز ذلك.

س: يكثر السؤال عن الأغاني المحللة والأغاني المحرمة، فهل نستطيع أن نقول أن الأغاني المحرمة هي تلك التي تثير الغرائز الجنسية الشهوانية وتدعو إلى الابتذال والميوعة أما الأغاني التي لا تثير الغرائز الهابطة والتي تسمو بالنفوس والأفكار إلى مستوى رفيع كالأغاني الدينية التي تتغنى بسيرة النبي محمد(ص) أو بمدح الأئمة(ع) أو الأغاني والأناشيد الحماسية، وأضرابها أغان محللة؟

بسمه تعالى

الغناء وحرام كله ، وهو على المختار ، الكلام اللهوي الذي يؤتى به بالألحان المتعارفة عند أهل اللهو واللعب ، ويلحق به ما لحرمة مقراءة القرآن الكريم والادعية المباركة بهذه الألحان ، وأما قراءة ماسوى ذلك من الكلام غير اللهوي ـ كالأناشيد والمداح ـ بالألحان الغنائية محرمة ما بنى على الاحتياط اللزومي .

س: في بعض الدول يصافح القادم كل الجالسين حتى النساء دون تلذذ ولو امتنع عن مصافحة النساء أثار سلوكه الاستغراب وغالبا ما يعده إساءة للمرأة واحتقارا لها مما ينعكس سلبا على نظرتهم إليه ، فهل يجوز مصافحتهن؟

لا يجوز ، وليعالج الموقف بلبس الكفوف مثلاً ، ولم يتيسر له ذلك وجب عليه الامتناع عن المصافحة وجرأ أشديداً لا يعمل عادة جارت لم عنده ، والله العالم .

س: هل يجوز تبادل الود والمحبة مع غير المسلم إذا كــان جاراً أو شريكاً في عمل أو ما شابه؟

بسم تعالى

إذا لم يكن يظهر للعداوة للاسلام والمسلمين بقول أو فعل فلا بأس بالقيام بمقتضيه الود والمحبة من البر والاحسان اليه قال الله تعالى (لا ينهاكم الله عن الذين لم يقاتلوكم في الدين ولم يخرجوكم من دياركم ان تبروهم وتقسطوا اليهم ان الله يحب المقسطين) .

س: هل يجوز التصدق على الكفار الفقراء كتابيين كــانوا أو غير كتابيين؟ وهل يثاب المتصدق على فعله هذا؟

لا بأس بالتصدق على من لم يصب العداوة للحق وأهله ويثاب المتصدق على فعله ذلك . والله العلم .

س: لقد بات معروفا ما للمخدرات من ضــــرر بليــغ علــى مستعملها أو على المجتمع ككل، سواء من ناحية الإدمــان عليها أم من النواحي الأخرى ولذلك فقد شن الأطباء ودور الرعاية الصحية حملة شديدة عليها وحاربتـــها القوانيــن المنظمة لشؤون المجتمع . فما هو رأي الشرع الشريف بها؟

بسمه تعالى

يحرم استعمالها مع ما يترتب عليه من الضرر البليغ سواء من جهة ادمانه او من جهة اخرى ، بل الاحوط لزوما الاجتناب عنها مطلقا الا في حالات الضرورة الطبية وعزها فتستعمل بمقدار ما تدعو اليه الضرورة والله العالم .

علي الحسيني

Appendix II

List of Main Harām Ingredients Used in the Manufacturing of Food[140]

Islamic Law has forbidden Muslims from consuming a number of ingredients. Since non-Muslim manufacturers of food are naturally not required to refrain from using those ingredients in their products, Muslims are required to be vigilant and careful —within the limits outlined by the sharí'a— in using those products.

We give below some information that was available for us regarding harām ingredients in food products. We have decided not to go into details in order to avoid —within the bounds of the sharí'a— complicating the life of a Muslim who is being tested by living in non-Muslims countries. The Islamic sharí'a, in spite of its meticulous and rigirous nature, is still a simple and linient code of practice; and, therefore, it is useful to point out two things right at the beginning.

Firstly, some raw ingredients used in manufacturing food and drink go through definite chemical transformations that radically change its original properties in the sense that it becomes, in common people's perception, a new and different matter. Such a transformation would remove it from the list of

---

[140] Quoted from *Dalílu 'l-Muslim fi Bilādi 'l-Ghurba*, p. 111 ff with modifications.

forbidden items, and this is known in the manuals of Islamic laws as *"al-istihālah"* which is one of the purifying agents according to the sharí'a.

For example, when an item derived from a harām animal source changes into a different item [through chemical transformation], then the latter product would become permissible.

Secondly, there are ingredients used in manufacturing food products that could have possibly come from a number of different sources, some of which are halāl and some are harām. In such cases, with no certain knowledge about the origin of such an item, it is not necessary to investigate and it is permissible to eat that doubtful item. (Of course, this principle does not apply to meat when there is doubt whether or not it is from an animal slaughtered according to the laws of Islam) So if you see in the list of ingredients "mono et diglycerides" which can originate from aminal fat or from vegetable oil, and the label does not specify that it comes from animal source, it is not incumbent on the person to investigate about it, and therefore it be considered halāl.

Now we shall provide some information about harām ingredients mentioning both their English as well as French names.

1. Oil & Shortening:

"Shortening" and "fat" ("matieres grasses" in French) is normally extracted from animal fat and sometimes vegetable oil is added to it. Whereas the word "lard" ("saindoux" in French) is used for fat of swine.

In American food products you will find the expression "vegetable shortening" which is not a totally factual statement because American laws permit the manufacturers to describe their product as having "vegetable shortening" as long as 80% to 90% of the shortening is vegetable based.

The phrases that entail satisfaction for us are "pure vegetable ghee" or "pure vegetable shortening" or "pure vegetable oil".

2. "Butter" ("beurre" in French) is made from milk and therefore there is no problem in using it.

3. Cheese: Contrary to the belief of some people, lard is not used in cheese. However, in the process of manufacturing cheese, an enzyme is used that is extracted from the stomach of animals (cow, calf, or pig). This enzyme is called "rennet," "renin," and "pepsin" ("presure" in French).

Since "pepsin" is the enzyme extracted from pigs, it is harām. However, the enzyme from cow or calf [i.e., rennet, renin] that was not slaughtered Islamically is by itself considered ritually pure (tāhir) and it is permissible to use. But the stomach becomes impure by coming into wet contact with other parts of the animal. So if one is unsure whether or not the najis container of enzyme was used in the process of making the cheese, it is permissible to eat it.

One should also be aware of other ingredients used in making cheese, some are vegetable based while others are chemically produced like microbic enzymes. There is no doubt in the purity as well as permissiblity of using these.

If there is doubt in the enzymes used in making cheese whether it was from natural sources or chemically produced, then you can consider it to be halāl.

4. As for "Gello" is concerned, it is used in manufacuring the gelatin. Mostly it is jellylike substance extracted from animal source. However, you can also obtain the Gello that is made from vegetable source and seaweeds.

5. As for non-alcoholic carbohydrate drinks like Coke, Pepsi, Seven Up, and Canada Dry, they do not contain anything from animal or alcoholic sources.

Note: In preparing the information in this Appendix, we have primarily relied on the write up of Dr. Ahmad Hasan Sakr of Chicago, USA, which is originally taken from the following sources:

1) Al-Mawsou's fi Uloom al-Tabi'a, Edward Chalib, Beirut 1965-66

2) Le Guide marabout de la peche en mer Michel van Haver - 1982 - FRANCE.

3) Les Poissons D'eau Douce Jiri Cihar 1976 – FRANCE.

4) Guide des Poissons D'eau Douce et Peche Bent J. Muvs et Preben Dahistrom 1981 – SUISSE.

5) Encyclopedie Illustree des Poissons Stanislav Frank – PARIS.

6) Encyclopedie du Monde Animal Tome 4 (Les Poissons et Les reptiles) Maurice Burton. Bibliotheque Marabout – PARIS.

* * *

Appendix III

Explanation on Ingredients and Preservatives Used in Food Products

In this Appendix, I am listing some of the ingredients and components that are usually added to the food. These ingredients come from vegeable soure or animals or are produced chemically. Since the labels on the food products do not list the origin of the ingredients, there is no way of classifying them as halāl or harām, except by referring to the manufacturers.

As for the ingredients that shall be listed here, I have tried to ascertain the suitability of their halāl use based on the information that I could gather. However, one should know that if an ingredient that is completely absorbed in a food product [and cannot be detected unless we are told by the manufacturer], it is not obligatory in the sharī'a to inquire about such ingredients to ascertain that they are free of harām substance. (See the chapter on "Food & Drink".)

1. Acetic Acid: It is found naturally in plant juices; it can also be produced chemically [from oil petroleum], and can also be derived from animal tissues.

If it is extracted from plant juices or from chemicals, there is no problem in using it in food products. But if it is extracted from animal tissues, the permissibility of using it depends on the animal having been slaughtered Islamically.   [If   the origin is unknown, one can still use it.]

2. Adipic Acid: It is from vegetable origin and it can also be produced from chemicals. Therefore, there is no problem in using it in food products.

3. Agar Agar: It comes from seaweed. It is used as a substitute for gelatin. Since it comes from vegetable origin, it is halāl.

4. Apocarotenal (C30) (E160e): It comes from orange. Sometimes it is used to melt gelatine or lard in water. If gelatine comes from an animal source (other than fish), it is not possible to use in food products.

5. Carmine / Cochineal (E120): It comes from insects and is used in coloring food items. It is halāl.

6. Casein: Its source is milk, and it is used in manufacturing cheese. It is precipitated by acid or by vegetable or animal enzymes. If vegetable enzymes were used in precipitation, it is halāl; but if animal enzymes were used then it cannot be considered halāl unless the animal was slaughtered Islamically or the process brought about a chemical transformation in casein.

7. Chocolate Liquor: This is a sweet liquid made from chocolate and used for its aroma. It is not the intoxicating or alcoholic drink known as "liquor;" and, therefore, there is no problem in using it.

8. Bextrose (Corn Syrup): Its source is starch and is used as sweetner and colouring agent in food products. Since it comes from vegetable source, there is no problem in using it.

9. Carbon Black (E153): [It is used for black colouring in confectionery] and is extracted from bones or meat or wood or plants. Since it can also be extracted from vegetable source, it is, in most cases, halāl. If it is extracted from an animal source,

one cannot consider it halāl unless he can ascertain that the animal was slaughtered Islamically or that it went through a process of chemical change.

10. Lecithin (E322): It is made from egg yolk but on a commercial basis it is made from soybeans and is therefore halāl.

11. Glycerine (E422) / Glyverol: Used as a solvent or humectant (maintains the desired level of moisture). It comes from beef fat or petroleum or vegetable. If it comes from chemical or vegetable source, it is halāl; but if it comes from animal source, it cannot be halāl, unless the animal was slaughtered Islamically or it went through the process of chemical transformation (istihalah).

12. Mono & Digylcerides: It comes from animal or vegetable source. If it comes from vegetable source, then it is halāl; if it comes from animal source, then it cannot be halāl unless the animal was slaughtered Islamically or it went through the process of chemical transformation.

13. Polyglycerol Easters of Fatty Acids (E476): Source: Fats and oils, animal or vegetable source. If they come from vegetable source, they are halāl; if they come from animal source, they cannot be halāl unless the animal was slaughtered Islamically or the acids went through the process of chemical transformation.

14. Monosodium Glutamate (E621): Source: Japaness seaweeds, sugar [plants, beets and corn]. It is used for enhancing flavor. It is halāl.

15. Gelatine: Derived from vegetable or animal source. If it is from vegetable source, there is no problem. But if it is from animal that was not slaughtered Islamically, it is halāl in view of the late Grand Ayatullāh as-Sayyid al-Khū'ī based on the chemical change *(istahālah)* that it goes through. As for the view of the Grand Ayatullāh as-Sayyid as-Sistāni, it is not

halāl because he believes that in chemical change the original components should be completely eliminated.

16. Guar Gum: It is used as stabilizer and thickener for spreads, syrup, etc. and is extracted from plants and is therefore halāl.

17. Lactic Acid: It is made from corn, soybeans, or sugarcane; it can also be made from chemicals. It is halāl.

18. Pectine: It is extracted from fruits and stems of plants. Commercially it is made from apples and is used for thickening jellies. It is halāl.

19. Pepsin: It comes from enzymes usually extracted from pig stomaches and obviously harām, unless it is chemically transformed into another substance.

20. Rennin (Rennet): Comes from animal enzymes usually derived from the membrane of the stomach of suckling calves. It can be made from vegetable enzyme or from chemical source. It is halāl.

21. Whey (in all forms): It comes from milk and is used as binder and flavouring agent. It is halāl.

* * *

Appendix IV

List and Pictures of Scale Fish[141]

The 1st column is in Latin, 2nd in English, 3rd in French, and 4th in Arabic.

---

[141] This list is based on *Dalīlu 'l-Muslim fi Bilādi 'l-Ghurba*, p. 93 ff.

أسماك ذوات فلس ذكرت في المتن

سمك سليمان / سلمون   Saumon

شبوط   Carpe

تروتة / اطروط   Truite

بوري (بلأ) (أكثر من مئة نوع)   Mullet

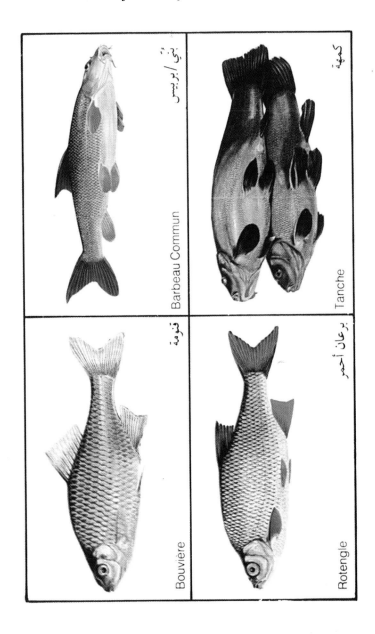

بني / بربس

Barbeau Commun

كمفية

Tanche

قريضة

Bouvière

برعان احمر

Rotengle

Zope

سمك بنقاء (نوع ثان)

Spirlin

سمك الترّس

Flet

Rasoir

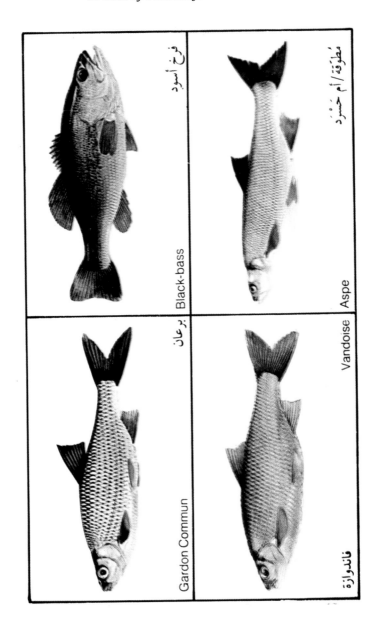

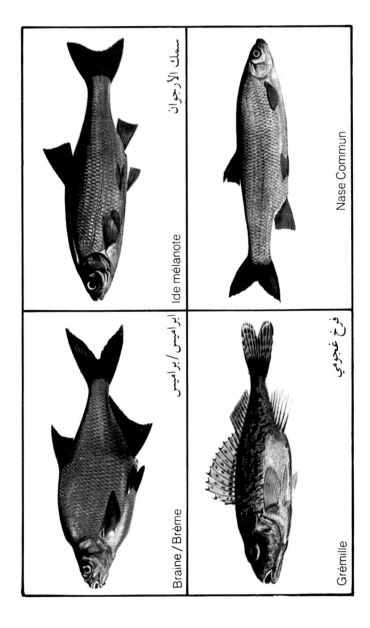

سمك الأرجوان

Ide mélanote

Nase Commun

ابر اميس / بر اميس

نرخ غجرمي

Braine / Brème

Grémille

Bibliography

The Holy Qur'ān

Al-Āmāli of Shaykh Muhammad bin al-Hasan at-Tûsi. Beirut: al-Wafā', 1981.

Al-Infāq fi Sabíli 'l-Lāh of Sayyid 'Izzud Din Bahrul 'Ulum. Beirut: Dar az-Zahrā', 1989.

Bihāru 'l-Anwār of Shaykh Muhammad Bāqir al-Majlisi. Beirut: al-Wafā', 1983.

Dalílu 'l-Muslim fi Bilādi 'l-Ghurba of Sayyid Najíb Yusûf and Shaykh Muhsin 'Atwa. Beirut: Dar at-Ta'āruf, 1990.

Ad-Dhunûb al-Kabíra of Sayyid 'Abdu 'l-Husayn Dastghayb. Beirut: ad-Dar al-Islāmiyya, 1988.

Al-Fatāwa al-Muyassara by the present writer. Beirut: Dar al-Mu'arrikh al-'Arabi, 1996.

Jāmi'u 's-Sa'ādāt of Shaykh Muhammad Mahdi an-Narāqi. Beirut: al-A'lami, 1988.

Al-Kawthar (premier issue). Qum: al-Majma' al-'Ālami li Ahli 'l-Bayt, 1994.

Khisāl of Shaykh Muhammad bin 'Ali Bābawayh al-Qummi. Tehran: Maktaba as-Sadûq, 1389.

Mafātihu 'l-Jinān of Shaykh 'Abbās al-Qummi. Beirut: al-A'lami, 1992.

Makārimu 'l-Akhlāq of Shaykh Hasan bin al-Fadl at-Tabrasi. Qum: Dar ash-Sharif ar-Radi, 1381.

Manāsiku 'l-Hajj of Sayyid 'Ali al-Husayni as-Sistani. Beirut: Dar al-Mu'arrikh al-'Arabi, 1994.

Man La Yahdhuruhu 'l-Faqíh of Shaykh Muhammad bin 'Ali bin al-Husayn bin Bābawayh. Beirut: Dar al-Adwā', 1985.

Al-Masā'ilu 'l-Muntakhaba of Sayyid 'Ali al-Husayni as-Sistāni. Beirut: Dar al-Mu'arrikh al-'Arabi. 1994.

Al-Masā'ilu 'sh-Shar'iyya of Sayyid Abul Qāsim al-Khû'í. Kuwait: Mu'assasa Muhammad Rafi' Mu'arrifi, 1996.

Minhāju 's-Sāliheen of Sayyid 'Ali al-Husayni as-Sistāni. Kuwait: Mu'assasa Muhammad Rafi' Mu'arrifi, 1996.

Mustadraku 'l-Wasā'il of Mirza Husayn an-Nuri. Beirut: Mu'assasa Ãli 'l-Bayt, 1987.

Nahju 'l-Balāgha of Imam 'Ali bin Abi Tālib (a.s.), edited by Subhi Sālih. Beirut: Dar al-Kitāb al-Lubnāni, 1982.

Qādatuna: Kayfa Na'rifuhum of Sayyid Muhammad Hadi al-Husayni al-Milani. Beirut: al-Wafā', 1407.

Qurbu 'l-Isnād of Shaykh 'Abdullah al-Himyari. Beirut: Mu'assasa Ãli 'l-Bayt, 1987.

Tafsílu Wasā'ili 'sh-Shí'a of Shaykh Muhammad bin Hasan al-Hurr al-'Ãmili. Qum: Mu'assasa Ãli 'l-Bayt, 1409.

Tahdhíbu 'l-Ahkām of Shaykh Muhammad bin Hasan at-Tusi. Beirut: Dar al-Adwā', 1985.

Thawābu 'l-A'māl wa 'Aqābu 'l-A'māl of Shaykh Muhammad bin 'Ali bin Muhammad bin Bābawayh al-Qummi. Beirut: Al-A'lami, 1983.

Al-Usûl mina 'l-Kāfi of Shaykh Muhammad bin Ya'qûb al-Kulayni. Beirut: Daru 'l-Adwā', 1985.

Az-Ziwāj fi 'l-Qur'ān wa 's-Sunna of Sayyid 'Izzud Din Bahrul 'Ulum. Beirut: Dar az-Zahra, 1984.

Az-Ziwāj al-Muwaqqat wa Dawruhu fi Halli Mushkilāti 'l-Jins of Sayyid Muhammad Taqi al-Hakim. Beirut: Dar al-Andulus, 1963.

* * *

NOTES

NOTES

NOTES

NOTES